Title: The Nazi Conspiracy: The Secret Plot to Kill Roosevelt, Stalin, and Churchill (Young Reader's Edition)

Author: Brad Meltzer

On-Sale Date: October 21, 2025

Format: Jacketed Hardcover

ISBN: 978-1-5461-2236-4

Price: $19.99 US

Ages: 9–12

Grades: 4–7

LOC Number: Available

Length: 384 pages

Trim: 5-1/2 x 8-1/4 inches

Classification: Juvenile Nonfiction: History / General / Military & Wars / Holocaust / Europe / United States / 20th Century / Social Science / Politics & Government / Social Topics / Violence / Biography & Autobiography / Presidents & First Families (US)

--------------- *Additional Formats Available* -------------

Ebook ISBN: 978-1-5461-2237-1

SCHOLASTIC FOCUS

An Imprint of Scholastic Inc.
557 Broadway, New York, NY 10012
For information, contact us at:
tradepublicity@scholastic.com

Dear Reader,

The President of the United States is hiding. That's how this young reader's adaptation of *The Nazi Conspiracy* begins in this all-true, nonfiction story about a real-life secret Nazi plot to kill Franklin Delano Roosevelt, Joseph Stalin, and Winston Churchill at the height of World War II—a triple assassination that would've changed the course of history.

So why bring this story to young readers? When it comes to Nazis and fanatics, well . . . it's a problem that sadly is more important than ever these days. According to the Anti-Defamation League, antisemitism in the modern era is at an all-time high. Indeed, the entire book looks back through history and asks the question, why are we still dealing with Nazis and antisemitism today?

Most important, I want kids to learn this lesson: As historians have pointed out, the Nazi movement did not begin with mass atrocities and death camps that we associate with the war. Nazism started gradually, with slogans, rallies, propaganda, and of course, book bans. And so, isn't it appropriate when we use books (and history) to fight back?

This is a story you won't believe—one that'll make sure you never look at World War II the same way again. Which side will our students pick? As always, throughout history, the answer is up to us.

See you in the history books,

Brad Meltzer

Brad Meltzer

THE NAZI CONSPIRACY

THE SECRET PLOT TO KILL ROOSEVELT, STALIN, AND CHURCHILL

YOUNG READER'S EDITION

ALSO BY

BRAD MELTZER

The First Conspiracy: The Secret Plot to Kill George Washington (with Josh Mensch)

The JFK Conspiracy: The Secret Plot to Kill Kennedy—and Why It Failed (with Josh Mensch)

The Lincoln Conspiracy: The Secret Plot to Kill America's 16th President —and Why It Failed (with Josh Mensch)

The Nazi Conspiracy: The Secret Plot to Kill Roosevelt, Stalin, and Churchill (with Josh Mensch)

The Lightning Rod

The Escape Artist

The House of Secrets

The President's Shadow

The Fifth Assassin

The Inner Circle

The Book of Lies

The Book of Fate

The Zero Game

The Millionaires

The First Counsel

Dead Even

The Tenth Justice

Heroes for My Daughter

Heroes for My Son

THE NAZI CONSPIRACY

THE SECRET PLOT TO KILL ROOSEVELT, STALIN, AND CHURCHILL

YOUNG READER'S EDITION

BRAD MELTZER

AND **JOSH MENSCH**

SCHOLASTIC FOCUS

NEW YORK

A Note to Readers:

The world map has changed a great deal over time. Boundaries and borders shift and new nations rise up and old ones get different (or sometimes, they return to old) names. This book uses the names of countries and territories as they were called in the early 1940s.

Library of Congress Cataloging-in-Publication Data available

ISBN 978-1-5461-2236-4

10 9 8 7 6 5 4 3 2 1 25 26 27 28 29

Printed in the U.S.A. 128

First edition, October 2025

Book design by Elizabeth B. Parisi and Abby Dening

Cover photo credits: ©: GK History Images/Alamy Stock Photo, Underwood Archives, Inc/Alamy Stock Photo, and Library of Congress

For Professor Tom Collier,
my history professor at the
University of Michigan,
who encouraged me decades ago
to dive into World War II

—B.M.

In memory of my father,
Steven H. Mensch
1943–2021

—J.M.

PROLOGUE

Tehran, Iran

— November 28, 1943 —

The President is hiding.

The street is lined with thousands of soldiers, extending for blocks on either side. They use their weapons and bodies to stop the people trying to push through to get a look.

Everyone turns toward the procession of approaching cars, a mix of military and civilian vehicles. At the center of the motorcade is a long, dark sedan, glistening in the bright sun. This is the car the soldiers have been ordered to protect.

Those who catch a glimpse see a tall, white-haired man

in the back seat. They crane their necks to get a better look at the President of the United States of America, Franklin Delano Roosevelt.

At least, that's who they *think* is inside.

The President is traveling to the Soviet embassy, a walled and heavily guarded complex of buildings in the north of the bustling city of Tehran, the capital of Iran. There he will meet with the two world leaders who are his allies in the war currently sweeping the globe: Joseph Stalin, Premier of the Union of Soviet Socialist Republics (the USSR, or Soviet Union), and Winston Churchill, Prime Minister of the United Kingdom.

Starting today is a conference that took nearly a year of planning. It will be the first time the "Big Three" come together in person.

Yet all is not as it seems.

Unbeknownst to onlookers and soldiers—and even to many within the motorcade of vehicles—the tall man in the back seat of the dark sedan is not, in fact, the President. He's a member of the US Secret Service, wearing a bulletproof vest and *pretending* to be the President.

At this moment, the *real* President Roosevelt is ducked down in the back of a small, dirty sedan, tearing through the winding backstreets of the city. While the sleek black

Presidential limousine is surrounded by armed vehicles and military personnel, the nondescript car transporting the actual President is escorted by a single jeep.

Why this elaborate deception?

The previous night, Soviet intelligence officials notified US security of an alarming discovery: In this city, which is under Allied control, undercover Nazi agents are on the move. Their mission, according to the Soviets, is to kill Franklin D. Roosevelt. And Winston Churchill. And Joseph Stalin. It's an almost unbelievable plot, breathtaking in its audacity. Right here in Tehran, during this momentous conference, Nazi agents will attempt to assassinate the Big Three.

For four years, World War II has been consuming the planet. Entire swathes of Europe, Asia, and North Africa have been utterly devastated. The suffering and loss of life are nearly incalculable and continue daily. Right now, there is no end in sight.

The driving force behind the war is an appalling ideology that took root in several nations but reached its most extreme and powerful form in Germany under the Nazi Party and its leader, Adolf Hitler.

Fascism.

Built on a twisted form of extreme patriotism, it's fueled

by racial hatred, mass propaganda, conspiracy theories, the demonizing of minority groups, and worship of the party leader. Under this ideology, Germany has turned toward hatred and violence—as have its principal allies, Italy and Japan. Together they are known as the Axis powers.

As the Nazis' empire—the Third Reich—expands and their power increases, they are committing atrocities that go far beyond the scope of ordinary warfare, targeting people they consider "undesirable": the Roma, the mentally ill and physically disabled, gay people, people of color, Poles and other Slavic people. Civilian populations, including children, are imprisoned and tortured, worked to death, or simply massacred.

Above all, the regime has directed its brutality toward one group that, from the very beginning, it has vilified and blamed: the Jewish people. To solve what they call "the Jewish problem" in Europe, Nazi leaders have, in the course of the war, created an apparatus of mass slaughter so horrific it will take years for the world to fully comprehend.

To fight back, the Allies have planned this long-anticipated meeting of the Big Three—the leaders of the United States of America, the United Kingdom, and the

Soviet Union—knowing that this meeting in Tehran represents the best and perhaps only chance for Allied powers to implement a military strategy to finally cripple Nazi Germany and put an end to the war that has caused such suffering around the world. Planning and executing this strategy will be a mammoth undertaking that will require global military coordination at an unprecedented scale.

Millions of lives depend on the success of this Tehran conference. Maybe even tens of millions. But if the Nazis have their way, these three men won't leave the city alive, and Allied hopes for victory will die with them.

It's not an exaggeration: The survival of nations is at stake.

And right now, President Roosevelt is ducked down, hiding in the back of a speeding car.

1

TWO YEARS EARLIER . . .

The White House, Washington, DC

— DECEMBER 7, 1941 —

President Franklin Delano Roosevelt is having breakfast in bed at the White House in Washington, DC. But this is no leisurely meal. He's surrounded by paperwork, and a telephone sits nearby.

He often starts the day this way. Since being stricken with polio two decades ago, he's been almost entirely without the use of his legs. He's found that working in bed while eating his breakfast is an efficient way to spend the morning.

This particular morning is a Sunday—December 7, 1941.

The President was up late the night before. US Naval Intelligence intercepted a top secret memo sent by the imperial government of Japan in Tokyo to the Japanese Ambassador in Washington, DC. When the Navy decoded and translated the memo, they discovered that it outlined the Japanese response to the latest round of American diplomacy, rejecting what Japan perceived to be the United States' unreasonable demands to stop Japan's expansion into China and various territories in the South Pacific region.

To put it bluntly, negotiations between the United States and Japan have collapsed.

This is the last thing the President wants. Now, his legs still under the covers, he is rereading the decoded memo and trying to understand its implications.

Minutes later, he receives another decrypted message, one that was sent at the same time as the first. This message instructs the Japanese Ambassador to deliver the first memo to American officials at 1 p.m. precisely. (They have it early because they intercepted the communication en route.) There is no explanation for why that time is so important. Even more ominously, the message instructs the Ambassador to destroy all confidential documents in the Japanese embassy.

This doesn't look good.

Time to get out of bed.

Once up, the President coordinates phone calls and meetings with key members of his foreign-policy and national-security staff. By midmorning, they're agreed that Japan is probably about to take military action against US-friendly interests in Southeast Asia. Perhaps they will attack British-controlled Singapore, or the US territory of Guam in the western Pacific, or seize the coveted oil fields of the Dutch East Indies. They might even attack the Philippines, an American protectorate. If they do, how should the United States react? Would these actions demand a military response?

The President's lunch of sandwiches taken at his desk is interrupted by a call from Frank Knox, the Secretary of the Navy. Knox's voice is shaking as he tells the President that the Pentagon "picked up a radio from Honolulu from our Commander-in-Chief of our forces there advising . . . that an air raid attack was on and that it was 'no drill.'" It appears, Knox continues after a pause, "like the Japanese have attacked Pearl Harbor."

Pearl Harbor? In Hawaii? That can't be right. The US naval base on the Hawaiian island of Oahu is considered invulnerable. It's also, based on its location, far from any

Japanese interests. Why would Japan attack Hawaii?

Shortly after Knox's call, Admiral Harold Stark, the Chief of Naval Operations, rings for the President and confirms the news: Japan has attacked Pearl Harbor. The base was entirely unprepared, and the results are catastrophic.

It's not for nothing that Roosevelt has earned a reputation for staying calm under pressure. So while his staff begins to react with near hysteria to the news from Hawaii, he remains in control. But with each new piece of terrible news, he shakes his head grimly and tightens his mouth even further.

And the terrible news keeps coming. The US naval base was caught totally unaware. The battle stations were mostly unmanned, and the ammunition was locked in storage. The ships in the harbor were sitting ducks.

The first wave of Japanese planes set their sights on Battleship Row. They attacked the USS *Oklahoma* first, with strafing guns and a pair of carefully aimed torpedoes. Massive explosions rocked the harbor when the fuel tanks ignited, and the huge vessel tilted as water flooded through the damaged hull. Minutes later, the battleship began sinking to the bottom of the harbor, pulling more than four hundred crew members down to their deaths.

Then the Japanese planes peeled off to strike the nearby

airfields. By the end of the attack, two battleships had been sunk, and several other battleships, destroyers, and cruisers were completely wrecked. The Navy's entire fleet of planes had been decimated. Well over two thousand American service members or staff were dead, and another thousand were seriously wounded. The harbor was an inferno of flames and smoke.

At 5 p.m., after a day of nonstop meetings and phone calls, Roosevelt slips away to his personal study next to the Oval Office. Tomorrow he will address both houses of Congress, and he needs to figure out what to say. The State Department has been working frantically, preparing a speech for him to review. Now it sits in front of him: fifteen pages long, containing a lengthy history of diplomatic relations with Japan and a detailed assessment of various military responses to the surprise attack.

Roosevelt tosses the papers aside. He may be addressing Congress, but he knows that his real audience is the American people. Rather than deliver a lecture on foreign policy, he needs to speak to a nation that has just been shocked to the core.

For that reason, his speech needs to be short, simple, and strong.

Every word counts.

. . .

America tried so hard to stay out of the war. They had recently lost many young soldiers in World War I, which was fought in Europe from 1914 to 1918 with Germany on one side and France and Great Britain on the other. The United States joined the French and British side in 1917.

The disillusion and confusion, felt especially by those who fought or lost loved ones, had a profound impact on a generation of Americans. After the troops came home, the overwhelming desire in the United States was to stay out of other countries' quarrels.

Nevertheless, the United States watched with a wary eye when, in the 1930s in Germany, the National Socialist Party and its *führer,* or leader, Adolf Hitler, came to power. The Nazi Party trafficked in a rage-filled patriotism that appealed to the fears and prejudices of Germany's rural and working classes. Hitler held huge rallies, where he worked his supporters into a frenzy with bombastic speeches that promised to restore Germany's fortunes. In those speeches, he spewed anger at "domestic enemies"—Jews and immigrants and minorities—whom he blamed for the nation's problems.

The Nazis demanded a return to imagined traditional

values and a renewed pride in an ethnically pure German race, which they called "Aryan." They distilled their ideas into a single term, "nationalism," which combined pride in one's country with a fear or hatred of immigrants, non-white minorities, and foreign influence. As Hitler declared in 1940, the concept of nationalism was "one strong new idea . . . which would make Germany great again."

Hitler and other Nazi Party leaders based many of their ideas on a conspiracy theory. They claimed that at the end of World War I, "globalists" conspired to force Germany's surrender and destroy its economy and culture, and that Jewish people were behind this conspiracy. Hatred of Jewish people was a principle that united the party and rallied its working-class base. In 1935, Germany's new "Nuremberg Laws" encoded white racial supremacy and stripped Jews of citizenship rights.

Increasingly, the Nazis used violence to eliminate political enemies and brutalize minorities. Hitler also launched an aggressive rearmament program to rebuild the German armies, using the threat of military force to annex nearby territories, such as Austria and the Sudetenland, which he claimed rightfully belonged to "the Fatherland" of Germany.

Roosevelt thought Nazism was a great danger and often

said so, declaring it the "enemy of all law, all liberty, all morality, all religion." But even after Hitler invaded Poland in September 1939—triggering declarations of war from the UK and France—Roosevelt was beholden to the powerful isolationists in Congress, as well as to the public who supported them.

Today, we all like to think we'd stand up to the Nazis, but back in 1940, for the most part, ordinary Americans were simply indifferent to European affairs. Even worse, in some parts of the country, a more sinister idea was taking hold. In 1930, roughly seven million people in America were German-born or second-generation German immigrants. While Hitler's rise in their home country appalled many, some German Americans embraced Nazi ideas. Throughout the northeastern and midwestern states, pro-Nazi organizations such as the Christian Front and the German American Bund emerged. These groups spread an Americanized Nazi message that combined conservative social values and flag-waving patriotism with appeals to the antisemitism and racism already prevalent throughout the country. Some pro-Nazi groups even established clubs and camps for young people, copying the Hitler Youth and the League of German Girls organizations in Germany. American boys and girls in New Jersey; Long Island, New York; and elsewhere learned the Hitler salute and could be seen marching through small towns wearing Nazi armbands.

On February 20, 1939, the German American Bund organized a rally in Madison Square Garden in New York City, which drew a crowd of twenty thousand. The stage was decorated with a huge poster depicting George Washington flanked by both Nazi swastikas and American flags. The first speaker of the night declared, to great applause, that "if George Washington were alive today, he would be friends with Adolf Hitler!" Later in the evening,

A rally at New York City's Madison Square Garden hosted by the pro-Nazi group the German American Bund. George Washington is flanked by both American flags and swastikas. (Alamy Stock Photo)

the keynote speech was delivered by the Bund's national leader, Fritz Kuhn, who declared that patriotic Americans had a duty to "fight for a Gentile America free of all atheistic Jewish Marxist elements." At one point, a young Jewish man in the audience jumped on the stage to protest the event. Bund members surrounded him, knocked him to the ground, then beat and kicked him in front of the crowd.

It wasn't just organizations like the Bund that supported Hitler. Some prominent Americans were also outspoken Nazi sympathizers. The renowned automaker Henry Ford, founder of the Ford Motor Company, held overtly antisemitic views and was not afraid to express them. In his newspaper, the *Dearborn Independent,* Ford wrote a screed with the headline "The International Jew: The World's Problem."

Other Americans were appalled by the Nazi threat and believed the United States should take a stronger stand against Hitler. Not surprisingly, the Jewish American community was at the forefront of this movement. Having experienced antisemitism firsthand, they understood how quickly it could grow and spread. In 1938, two Jewish comic book creators, Jerry Siegel and Joe Shuster, came up with Superman, a character who used his extraordinary strength to save people in desperate situations. And in 1941, two other working-class Jews, Joe Simon and Jack Kirby, created Captain America as a direct response to Nazism. The first issue depicted the muscle-bound hero, wearing red, white, and blue, punching out Adolf Hitler. It was an overt political statement at a time when most Americans opposed entry into the war.

But it was fantasy to think that the United States would stand up to defend the Jewish people and other vulnerable populations from Nazi violence. The truth was that most Americans did not know or care about the threat of Nazism in Europe. And they simply didn't want to get involved in another foreign conflict.

On the evening of November 9, 1938, now known as *Kristallnacht*, or the "Night of Broken Glass," violence erupted in Germany. The Nazi Party's paramilitary force, the Sturmabteilung (SA), instigated a nationwide pogrom against Jewish people and riled up German citizens to participate. Attackers destroyed 267 synagogues and ransacked thousands of Jewish hospitals, schools, and businesses. The SA beat, arrested, and sometimes even killed helpless Jewish civilians.

Kristallnacht was the first undeniable evidence of Nazi violence against Jewish people that reached the wider

The first issue of Captain America, encouraging the United States to stand up to Nazi Germany and protect Jewish populations. (Captain America, March #1 1941/Venimages/Alamy Stock Photo)

international public. As a result of it, Jewish Americans began pushing for the United States to confront the scourge of Nazism directly and with military force. But even if he'd wanted to, Roosevelt couldn't have taken the country to war. Given public opinion, Congress wouldn't have authorized it. Even after Hitler conquered most of Central Europe, and after France fell to the Nazis in spring 1940, the United States still didn't enter the conflict.

Short of committing troops, Roosevelt did what he could. In March 1941, he signed the landmark Lend-Lease bill, authorizing the United States to "lend" armaments and military supplies to the UK at no cost. The policy was met with internal political resistance—"Lending war equipment is a good deal like lending chewing gum. You don't want it back," the isolationist Senator Robert Taft argued—but this program would prove critical to the UK's survival.

Still, as of April 1941, a whopping 81 percent of Americans were opposed to the United States entering the conflict. It would take an extraordinary event to change their minds. Now, in December of 1941, it has arrived.

2

In the end, it wasn't Germany that drew the United States into the war.

It was Japan. Inspired in part by the rise of the Nazis, Japan adopted its own doctrine of racial superiority that placed the Japanese above all other Asian peoples. For the Japanese, this belief justified carrying out atrocities against the Koreans, the Chinese, and other groups they deemed racially inferior to themselves.

In August 1937, Japan launched a brutal attack on China, first conquering the city of Shanghai and then marching to the capital city of Nanjing. There, the Japanese army reportedly slaughtered as many as two hundred thousand Chinese civilians, including children. The invasion and the atrocities that followed were met with international criticism and led to an official American policy of deterrence against further Japanese expansion. The US Navy's Pacific Fleet, headquartered in Hawaii and with bases in the Philippines and elsewhere in the South Pacific, would be that deterrent.

In September 1940, Japan signed the Tripartite Pact with Germany and Italy, formally allying with the European fascists. Japan's pact with Hitler was a strategic gamble. Fully aware that the American public didn't want to get involved in another war, the Japanese hoped their alliance with Nazi Germany would deter the United States from interfering with their expansion. Instead, it only convinced America to stand strong against Japanese aggression while imposing tough sanctions, including an oil embargo to cripple Japanese naval operations.

Despite the animosity and the sanctions, Roosevelt never imagined that Japan would provoke a full-scale war with the United States. "It would not do this country any good nor Japan any good, but both of them harm to get into war," he told the Japanese Ambassador in Washington. Increasingly preoccupied with the situation in Europe,

Roosevelt believed that when it came to Asia, all parties would reach an agreement to avoid a trans-Pacific war.

Japan viewed it differently. Their militarist leaders were set on continuing Japanese expansion, and they decided that a clash with the United States was inevitable. Better to strike now while they were in a strong position. If they waited for diplomacy, the delay would allow the United States to continue to expand its navy, and Japan would lose the upper hand.

With the element of surprise on their side, Japanese leaders calculated they could debilitate the US naval fleet in one overwhelming strike—and when America saw Japan's power, they'd back off and stop policing the Pacific. For that reason, in the summer and fall of 1941, as Japanese envoys continued their facade of diplomacy, their country's military leaders were planning one of the most audacious surprise attacks in world history.

"War! Oahu Bombed by Japanese Planes."

So declares the oversized headline in the evening edition of the *Honolulu Star-Bulletin,* hours after the attack. The Honolulu press gets the news out first, but within minutes, radio broadcasts and other newspapers around the country begin filing their stories. By Monday, December 8,

Honolulu Star-Bulletin 1st EXTRA

Evening Bulletin, Est. 1882, No. 11279 Hawaiian Star, Vol. XLVIII, No. 15309 — 8 PAGES—HONOLULU, TERRITORY OF HAWAII, U. S. A., SUNDAY, DECEMBER 7, 1941—8 PAGES — PRICE FIVE CENTS

WAR!

(Associated Press by Transpacific Telephone)

SAN FRANCISCO, Dec. 7.—President Roosevelt announced this morning that Japanese planes had attacked Manila and Pearl Harbor.

OAHU BOMBED BY JAPANESE PLANES

SIX KNOWN DEAD, 21 INJURED, AT EMERGENCY HOSPITAL

Attack Made On Island's Defense Areas

By UNITED PRESS

WASHINGTON, Dec. 7.—Text of a White House announcement detailing the attack on the Hawaiian islands is:

"The Japanese attacked Pearl Harbor from the air and all naval and military activities on the island of Oahu, principal American base in the Hawaiian islands."

Oahu was attacked at 7:55 this morning by Japanese planes.

The Rising Sun, emblem of Japan, was seen on plane wing tips.

Wave after wave of bombers streamed through the clouded morning sky from the southwest and flung their missiles on a city resting in peaceful Sabbath calm.

According to an unconfirmed report received at the governor's office, the Japanese force that attacked Oahu reached island waters aboard two small airplane carriers.

It was also reported that at the governor's office either an attempt had been made to bomb the USS Lexington, or that it had been bombed.

CITY IN UPROAR

Within 10 minutes the city was in an uproar. As bombs fell in many parts of the city, and in defense areas the defenders of the islands went into quick action.

Army intelligence officers at Ft. Shafter announced officially shortly after 9 a. m. the fact of the bombardment by an enemy but long previous army and navy had taken immediate measures in defense.

"Oahu is under a sporadic air raid," the announcement said.

"Civilians are ordered to stay off the streets until further notice."

CIVILIANS ORDERED OFF STREETS

The army has ordered that all civilians stay off the streets and highways and not use telephones.

Evidence that the Japanese attack has registered some hits was shown by three billowing pillars of smoke in the Pearl Harbor and Hickam field area.

All navy personnel and civilian defense workers, with the exception of women, have been ordered to duty at Pearl Harbor.

The Pearl Harbor highway was immediately a mass of racing cars.

A trickling stream of injured people began pouring into the city emergency hospital a few minutes after the bombardment started.

Thousands of telephone calls almost swamped the Mutual Telephone Co., which put extra operators on duty.

At The Star-Bulletin office the phone calls deluged the single operator and it was impossible for this newspaper, for sometime, to handle the flood of calls. Here also an emergency operator was called.

HOUR OF ATTACK—7:55 A. M.

An official army report from department headquarters, made public shortly before 11, is that the first attack was at 7:55 a. m.

Witnesses said they saw at least 50 airplanes over Pearl Harbor.

The attack centered in the Pearl Harbor, Army authorities said:

"The rising sun was seen on the wing tips of the airplanes."

Although martial law has not been declared officially, the city of Honolulu was operating under M-Day conditions.

It is reliably reported that enemy objectives under attack were Wheeler field Hickam field, Kaneohe bay and naval air station and Pearl Harbor.

Some enemy planes were reported short shot down.

The body of the pilot was seen in a plane burning at Wahiawa.

Oahu appeared to be taking calmly after the first uproar of queries.

ANTIAIRCRAFT GUNS IN ACTION

First indication of the raid came shortly before 8 this morning when antiaircraft guns around Pearl Habor began sending up a thunderous barrage.

At the same time a vast cloud of black smoke arose from the naval base and also from Hickam field where flames could be seen.

BOMB NEAR GOVERNOR'S MANSION

Shortly before 9:30 a bomb fell near Washington Place, the residence of the governor. Governor Poindexter and Secretary Charles M. Hite were there.

It was reported that the bomb killed an unidentified Chinese man across the street in front of the Schuman Carriage Co. where windows were broken.

C. E. Daniels, a welder, found a fragment of shell or bomb at South and Queen Sts. which he brought into the City Hall. This fragrent weighed about a pound.

At 10:05 a. m. today Governor Poindexter telephoned to The Star-Bulletin announcing he has declared a state of emergency for the entire territory.

He announced that Edouard L. Doty, executive secretary of t he major disaster council, has been appointed director under the M-Day law's provisions.

Governor Poindexter urged all residents of Honolulu to remain off the street, and the people of the territory to remain calm.

Mr. Doty reported that all major disaster council wardens and medical units were on duty within a half hour of the time the alarm was given.

Workers employed at Pearl Harbor were ordered at 10:10 a. m. not to report at Pearl Harbor.

The mayor's major disaster council was to meet at the city hall at about 10:30 this morning.

At least two Japanese planes were reported at Hawaiian department headquarters to have been shot down.

One of the planes was shot down at Ft. Kamehameha and the other back of the Wa-

Turn to Page 2, Column 1

Hundreds See City Bombed

Hundreds of Honolulans who hurried to the top of Punchbowl soon after bombs began to fall, saw spread out before them the whole panaroma of surprise attack and defense.

Far off over Pearl Harbor the white sky was polka-dotted with anti-aircraft smoke.

Rolling away from the navy base were billowing clouds of ugly black smoke. Sometimes a burst of flame reddened the black sources of the smoke.

Out from the silver-surfaced mouth of the harbor a flotilla of destroyers streamed to battle, smoke pouring from their stacks.

Turn to Page 2, Column 3

Names of Dead and Injured

The city emergency hospital reported at 10:30 a list of 6 killed and 21 injured.

The complete list will be carried later. Here is a partial list:

Peter Lopes, 34, of 2041 Kamanaiki St., was reported at 9:30 a. m. to be in serious condition from wounds in the upper abdomen.

Bernice Gouveia, 12, 2708 Kalihi St., is suffering from a mangled thigh, lacerations on the right leg and left arm.

A Portuguese girl, unidentified, 10 years old, died on arrival from puncture wounds.

Another victim who died on arrival was Frank Ohashi, 29, 2735 Kamanaiki St., from puncture wounds in the chest.

Cecelia Broadly, 38, Moanalua gardens, was released from the hospital after treatment for lacerations.

Three were reported injured and one reported killed from the bomb that fell at Fort and School Sts.

Schools Closed

All schools on Oahu, both public and private, will remain closed until further notice. Edouard L. Doty, territorial director of civilian defense, announced at 11 a. m. today. This does not apply elsewhere in the territory.

Editorial

HAWAII MEETS THE CRISIS

Honolulu and Hawaii will meet the emergency of war today as Honolulu and Hawaii have met emergencies in the past—coolly, calmly and with immediate and complete support of the officials, officers and troops who are in charge.

Governor Poindexter and the army and navy leaders have called upon the public to remain calm; for civilians who have no essential business on the streets to stay *off*; and for every man and woman to do his duty.

That request, coupled with the measures promptly taken to meet the situation that has suddenly and terribly developed, will be needed.

Hawaii will do its part—as a loyal American territory.

In this crisis, every difference of race, creed and color will be submerged in the one desire and determination to play the part that Americans always play in crisis.

BULLETIN

Additional Star-Bulletin extras today will cover the latest developments in this war move.

The front page of the December 7, 1941, edition of the *Honolulu Star-Bulletin* announces America's entry into World War II following the Japanese military's bombing of Pearl Harbor. (Shawshots/Alamy Stock Photo) every press outlet in the nation is struggling to keep up with the flood of new details. The attack on Pearl Harbor, it turns out, isn't a stand-alone event; it is part of a coordinated Japanese assault across the Pacific, with surprise attacks on Hong Kong, Malaya, the Philippines, Wake Island, and Guam. People want answers. Why was the US Navy caught so unprepared? What does this mean for the war in Europe? How will the country respond to this attack on a US territory?

It's time to address the nation.

At 12:30 p.m., President Roosevelt's aides wheel him to a car waiting at the East Gate of the White House. His advisers have urged him to travel in a military vehicle with an escort—better to be safe considering the recent attack. Roosevelt refuses, insisting that he ride in a convertible with the top down. He's the President of the American people, not some shadowy military dictator who sneaks around.

Shortly after 1 p.m., the car arrives at its destination: the US Capitol, where the US Senate and the House of Representatives are gathered. As the President enters the chamber, members of both bodies rise in a standing ovation. Roosevelt has many enemies in Congress, but today the lawmakers put their differences aside.

When it comes to speeches and other public events, Roosevelt is usually wheeled or lifted onto stages and lecterns, to hide his disability and have him appear before crowds looking like any other public figure. Today is different: The President makes a point of getting to the podium by himself. To do so, he has to put all his weight on his arm braces and drag his legs along the floor. Given the already heightened emotion in the room, it is a display of vulnerability and courage that has everyone catching their breath. The President could easily stumble or fall to the ground—as he has done in the past.

He makes it to the podium without falling. Then, using his arms, he props himself up to his full height of six foot two and begins to speak in a clear, methodical tone. "Yesterday, December 7, 1941—a date which will live in infamy—the United States of America was suddenly and deliberately attacked by naval and air forces of the Empire of Japan."

Roosevelt doesn't use any arm gestures—he needs to keep both hands on the podium to support his weight and can only use head movements for emphasis. "The attack yesterday on the Hawaiian Islands has caused severe damage to American naval and military forces," he continues. Then, after a pause, "I regret to tell you that very many American lives have been lost."

It's now a full day after the attack, and families around the country have been notified that a loved one has perished. In the days ahead, many more will receive the same news.

"I believe that I interpret the will of the Congress and of the people when I assert that we will not only defend ourselves to the uttermost but will make it very certain that this form of treachery shall never again endanger us."

This line gets a round of applause, and then a standing ovation. It's a clear signal to Congress what action they must take. In conclusion, Roosevelt asks, officially, that Congress authorize a state of war "between the United States and the Japanese Empire."

The speech lasts barely six minutes, including breaks for applause.

Within about half an hour of Roosevelt leaving the podium, the Senate votes 82–0 to pass a declaration of war and the House of Representatives 388–1.

The United States is now at war with Japan.

3

Buckinghamshire, United Kingdom

— DECEMBER 7, 1941 —

News travels fast.

It takes just a few hours for the story of the attack on Pearl Harbor to travel over 7,200 miles from Hawaii to reach a man sitting at a dining table in a stately home in the English countryside. Sixty-seven years old, he's short and squat, somewhat round in the belly, with wide, jowly cheeks and piercing eyes under a perpetually furrowed brow. For two years, he's shouldered the burden of defending the United Kingdom against the aggression and military occupation of Nazi Germany.

Winston Churchill.
(Library of Congress)

He's Winston Churchill, the Prime Minister of the United Kingdom and First Lord of the Admiralty, and, for once, he is speechless.

This in itself is unusual. Under normal circumstances, words rarely stop pouring from Churchill's mouth. His oratory, debating skills, and sharp wit are legendary, as is his appetite for food, drink, and cigars. Despite his unhealthy habits and his advancing age, he possesses an almost inexhaustible energy. He sometimes works straight through the night, even until dawn, especially if he's been refreshed by his cherished midday bath.

When he became Prime Minister in May 1940, Nazi Germany had already annexed or occupied Austria, parts of Czechoslovakia, Poland, Denmark, Norway, Belgium, the Netherlands, and Luxembourg, using brutal force. In his first speech as Prime Minister, delivered to the House of Commons on May 13, 1940, Churchill summarized his mission:

> *You ask, what is our policy? I can say: It is to wage war, by sea, land and air, with all our might and with all the strength that God can give us; to wage war against a monstrous tyranny, never surpassed in the dark, lamentable catalogue of human crime. That is our policy. You ask, what is our aim? I can answer in one word: It is victory, victory at all costs, victory in spite of all terror . . . for without victory, there is no survival.*

As for his own role, he said simply, "I have nothing to offer but blood, toil, tears and sweat." Almost immediately, Churchill came to embody the British war effort.

The problem was, he was presiding over a disaster. Just five weeks after he became Prime Minister, France surrendered to Nazi forces. Until that moment, France was supposed to have the largest military in the world. The Germans crushed it with ease.

In the face of such strength, Italy joined the war on Germany's side. Like Germany, Italy was ruled by a fascist dictator, Benito Mussolini, known as *Il Duce* ("the leader"). That left the British.

They were supported, as much as was possible, by their Commonwealth colonies and dominions—countries like Australia, Canada, India, and the Caribbean islands—but they were essentially alone in Europe. The English Channel, guarded by the Royal Navy and the Royal Air Force, was all that separated them from invasion by Nazi ground forces.

Barely a month into Churchill's term as Prime Minister, the UK's very existence was in doubt. In July 1940, the German air force—the Luftwaffe—launched an aerial campaign against the UK, called a blitzkrieg, which would come to be known as the Blitz. Their bombers aimed for British cities, targeting civilians to inflict maximum suffering and force surrender.

Churchill desperately needed a strategic partner, and his great hope was that the United States would enter the war. But despite Churchill's insistent pleading—and he could be very insistent—Roosevelt would not, or could not, bring the United States into the war. All Churchill could do was hope that something—anything—would change America's mind.

When the news of Japan's attack on Hawaii reaches him, Churchill is in the middle of a dinner with several military advisers as well as two American diplomats. They are sitting at the dining table in Chequers, the country house of the British Prime Minister. The radio is on in the background, and the BBC radio announcer reads a special report: "The Japanese Imperial Navy have bombed Pearl Harbor."

At first, Churchill and his aides are confused. The designation "Pearl Harbor" isn't well known outside the United States. The two Americans present know exactly what the announcer means, but still they're confused by the broadcast. In good English fashion, the news is confirmed by none other than the butler, who has been listening to the radio in the servants' quarters. He informs them that the Japanese have in fact bombed the US naval base in Hawaii.

The whole room is stunned.

For two years, Churchill has yearned for a partner. And he has prayed for the United States to be that partner. This might be the moment when the United States enters the war. Standing up from the table, he throws down his napkin and rushes out of the room. Something must be done—but what? Send ships to the South Pacific?!

It's the US Ambassador to the UK, John Winant, who steadies him. They cannot conduct foreign policy based on a radio report. Winant suggests that first they call Washington and confirm what happened. Moments later, he has Roosevelt on the line. Churchill takes the receiver. "Mr. President, what's this about Japan?" he asks.

"Yes, the Japanese attacked Pearl Harbor," Roosevelt replies. Then, after a pause, he speaks the most welcome words that Churchill has heard since the start of the war: "I guess we're in the same boat now."

In the same boat.

It sounds like the United States is going to war.

Churchill is careful not to display happiness in front of the Americans. After all, the United States has just suffered a tragedy. But after two years with his nation on the verge of extinction, he is flooded, as he later put it, with "the greatest joy."

Still, it would be premature to celebrate. The next day, President Roosevelt will ask Congress for a declaration of war—but against Japan only. He doesn't request the same against Germany or Italy. If he did, Congress would probably not grant it.

When it comes to the United States going to war against *Germany,* that's a decision that won't be made by Winston Churchill, or by Franklin Roosevelt. It will be made by a very different person, several thousand miles away.

4

The Wolf's Lair, East Prussia

— DECEMBER 7, 1941 —

Someone has to tell the Führer.

The news of Japan's attack on Pearl Harbor comes as a complete surprise to the Nazis, just as it does to everyone else. Hitler hears the news at the *Wolfsschanze*—"The Wolf's Lair"—a secluded fortress in East Prussia (now Poland). Lately, rather than operating from the German capital, Berlin, he has been spending more time at this remote forest headquarters. He's obsessed with the day-to-day operations of the German armies on the Russian front, and being here allows him to focus.

His decision to invade the Soviet Union six months

ago, in June 1941, was Hitler's greatest gamble yet, and, he believes, his masterstroke. Conquering the Slavic people, whom Hitler believed were "inferior"; eliminating the scourge of Communism; securing the rich resources in the Soviet Union; and punishing the large Jewish populations of the east were all components in Hitler's grand design.

To launch the invasion, which they called Operation Barbarossa, Germany amassed one of the largest fighting forces in human history. With ruthless speed, the infantry and tank divisions of the German army, the Wehrmacht, stormed eastward while the Luftwaffe rained destruction from above. Within a few months, Nazi troops were approaching Leningrad and Moscow.

However, all did not go according to plan.

Given how quickly German armies swept through Central and Western Europe in 1940, Hitler imagined that the Soviet Union would also crumble with ease. At first, the Wehrmacht performed as expected, with millions of troops and tanks advancing many hundreds of miles over the summer and decimating everything in their path, including any divisions of the Soviet army that tried to repel it. Yet after this spectacular beginning, progress began to stall. German troops were becoming exhausted, and the task of keeping millions of soldiers fed and equipped over the vast Soviet terrain was logistically overwhelming for military leaders.

The Soviet Union had started the war on the same side as Nazi Germany, joining the Germans in the brutal conquest of Poland in 1939. It was only when Hitler broke his alliance with them and invaded their own country that they decided they had a problem with the Nazi agenda. When Stalin recovered from the shock of Hitler's betrayal, tired German troops started to encounter a stiffer and better-organized Soviet resistance. Then, just as the German offensive was beginning to falter, the Germans came up against the toughest enemy of all: "General Frost"—Russia's long, brutally cold winter.

Hitler had been so sure that he would secure victory over the Soviets by early fall that he and his military leaders had simply failed to equip the soldiers in the infantry and tank divisions with proper winter gear. Soon, the freezing-cold troops were dying of frostbite before they even encountered the enemy.

Now, with winter hitting full force, Hitler has no choice but to pull his armies back to defensive positions. This is the first real setback for Nazi forces since the war began. Hitler is worried that the setback makes him look weak, and, for the mighty Führer, nothing is worse than looking weak.

When he first hears the news about Pearl Harbor, Hitler is just as astonished as Churchill and Roosevelt were. Because of the absolute secrecy required for the surprise attack, Japan didn't notify its own allies of the plan.

Some of the other Nazi leaders at the Wolf's Lair are concerned. Given the setback in Russia, the last thing they need is for the United States to enter the war. But Hitler sees it as great news. Pearl Harbor is a welcome diversion from Russia. He "slapped his thighs with delight as news of the report was brought to him," according to one Nazi official's account. The Führer's excitement is contagious—at least, everyone is required to follow along—and the Wolf's Lair is "caught up in an ecstasy of rejoicing." Nazi Foreign Minister Joachim von Ribbentrop is soon "jumping for joy about the Japanese attack on the United States."

Four days from now, Hitler is scheduled to deliver a major speech to the Reichstag, the German parliament. The timing couldn't be better. The speech will provide the perfect opportunity for him to divert the world's attention from his setbacks on the Eastern Front and onto Pearl Harbor.

Adolf Hitler addressing the Reichstag four days after Pearl Harbor. His speech will alter the course of the war. (© CBW/Alamy Stock Photo)

Some of his ministers urge caution. With Germany's armed forces already extended to the east in the Soviet Union and battling with Great Britain to the west, the last thing they need is another enemy—in this case, the United States. Perhaps Hitler's strategy, they suggest, should be to support Japan in its conflict with the Americans but to not provoke direct conflict between the United States and Germany. Thus far, the United States has only declared war on Japan, and perhaps it's best to keep it that way.

Hitler angrily rejects any such idea. For starters, he does not fear the United States. It is, he believes, fundamentally weak, having betrayed its white racial heritage to become a "mongrel nation of lesser races." He also believes that he must always be the aggressor, the one to dictate events. Without consulting or even informing his military leaders, he instructs his foreign ministry to draw up a formal declaration of war against the United States.

On December 11, three days after Franklin Roosevelt addressed the US Congress, Hitler enters the Kroll Opera House in Berlin, where hundreds of members of the Reichstag are seated. Because he has already had murdered or arrested any members of parliament who dared oppose him, today he'll be speaking to the faithful. Cries of *"Sieg Heil!"* fill the room as he approaches the podium and begins to speak.

He starts with an update on the war, extolling the successes of the German army on the Eastern Front. When he mentions Germany's casualty numbers, he gives figures that are basically false. One of Hitler's methods is to say only what is flattering to himself and the Nazi regime. And if the facts are not flattering, he lies. Midway through the speech, he mentions the American President in a snide tone. He then proceeds to attack Roosevelt's character and his abilities, referring to his "ignorance" and "narrow intellect." Roosevelt, he declares, is, like Churchill, part of the "Anglo-Saxon–Jewish–Capitalist World." The German people must stand behind their Führer and fight against these foreigners and against the Jews. After massive applause, Hitler makes it official: Germany will declare war on the United States.

With this declaration, the global stage is irrevocably set. Nazi Germany, Italy, and Japan are at war with the UK, the Soviet Union, and the United States.

Churchill. Stalin. Roosevelt. These are Hitler's enemies, and Germany's, too.

5

Tehran, Iran

— JANUARY 1943 —

He knows how to blend in.

In the city of Tehran, Iran, life doesn't appear much different from how it was three or four years ago, before the war. The markets are still buzzing with customers. The cafés and the shops are still doing brisk business. The busy mix of cars, bicycles, and pedestrians still crowds the narrow streets.

Iran doesn't have the option of staying neutral in the war. It shares a northern border with Russia, and right now it's being monitored by a combination of Soviet, British, and American forces. That's why this slender man in his late twenties who sometimes visits Tehran's cafés and markets must keep a very low profile. In fact, he needs to wear a disguise.

His name is Franz Mayr. But only a handful of people in the city know him by this name. For everyone else, he uses an alias.

Why so much secrecy?

Franz Mayr is a Nazi.

What's he doing in Tehran?

Four years earlier, when the war began, Mayr was eager, like many young German men, to serve the Nazi cause. He trained as a military signals operator, but his superiors soon transferred him to an area better suited to his abilities—intelligence—and he joined the Sicherheitsdienst (SD), the Nazi intelligence organization. Unlike Germany's established military intelligence agency, the Abwehr, the SD was part of the Nazi Party and answered only to Adolf Hitler.

Within its entry-level ranks, Mayr made friends with another young recruit named Roman Gamotha. The two signed up for "Middle East duty," unaware of what this meant or where it would take them. With little advance training, they were sent to the neutral nation of Iran and told to assume aliases and to operate in the country on behalf of Germany. In other words, they would be Nazi spies.

Later, a British intelligence file described the situation the two young agents found themselves in:

> The SD were unable to give them any accurate information about the country. Nor did they receive any training in intelligence work, W/T [wireless transmitters] or sabotage methods . . . They were given no contacts, no definite assignments, nor were there any courier arrangements. [The head of the SD section] merely told them first to get to Persia and there to become acquainted with the country. Instructions would follow.

Those instructions never arrived.

The two young agents made their way to the Iranian capital of Tehran and connected with the German embassy there. They were given cover jobs in a trading firm and had the freedom to work as agents-at-large in the city.

At first, despite their unfamiliarity with the language

and local customs, life was not too hard for the spies. At the start of the war, Iran and its government were pro-German. The country's leader, Reza Shah, looked up to Hitler and was eager to learn from and adopt elements of Nazism. Hitler responded favorably to Reza Shah's fawning attention and sought to cement a relationship. For one, Iran had oil, and Hitler needed oil to feed his growing war machine. Second, the geography of Iran provided many strategic benefits.

Indeed, it was Iran's geographic position that would suddenly transform Mayr's and Gamotha's lives. When Hitler attacked the Soviet Union in June 1941, one of the Allies' top priorities was to send arms and supplies from the United States and the UK to the Soviet Union. They quickly realized that the Trans-Iranian Railway, which ran through Iran from the Persian Gulf to the Caspian Sea, was the best route to transport supplies. After that, they wasted no time. In August 1941, a combined force of Soviet and British soldiers crossed into Iran from the north and east, quickly forcing a surrender of the pro-German government. Hitler's friend, Reza Shah, fled the country and was replaced by his son, Mohammad Reza Pahlavi, who, unlike his father, was willing to cooperate with the Allies.

For the two German spies, everything changed

overnight. Suddenly, they found themselves in enemy territory. If they were outed as Nazi agents, they would be arrested or killed. And because the Allies had cut off communication channels between Iran and Germany, they had no way to contact their superiors in Berlin. "The situation inside the country is getting worse and worse," Mayr wrote in his diary on June 28, 1942. "Yesterday, radio and newspaper gave warnings again not to give shelter to anyone belonging to the Axis powers. The state police threatened severe punishment for this."

The duo received no communications whatsoever. Their handlers in Berlin had apparently either forgotten all about them or assumed they were dead. As Mayr put it, they were living "the life of an enemy in the midst of the enemy" where there was "danger every hour and every minute of every day and every night."

Shortly after the Allied invasion, Roman Gamotha decided to abandon Middle East duty and fled Tehran. His plan was to escape over the border into neutral Turkey. Mayr refused to flee. He had built a resistance movement of pro-Nazi sympathizers ready to rise up against the Allies when the opportunity arose.

For most of 1942, Mayr shuffled between safehouses, using different aliases and disguises, always on the move.

For several months, he lived in the attic of a German sympathizer's home—until British officials raided the house. Fortunately for Mayr, he wasn't there, although the British did seize his papers and diary. From that point on, he knew that the British were onto him.

Through all these ups and downs, Mayr never wavered from his mission. He remained a dedicated German agent, devoted to the cause.

It wasn't just his loyalty to the Führer that kept him in Tehran.

Franz Mayr, the Nazi spy, was in love.

He had met Lili Sanjari shortly after he arrived in Tehran. She worked for the trading firm where he and Gamotha had been given cover jobs. Some of her childhood years had been spent in Berlin, and perhaps this connection to Mayr's homeland is what drew the two together. When the Allies took over and Mayr was forced to go underground, the relationship went underground as well. Sanjari could only see him in secret, and they spent long periods apart because any connection with him would put both her and her family at risk.

So, at the start of 1943, life has grown complicated for Franz Mayr. He's juggling multiple disguises and aliases, working as an undercover agent in a foreign city controlled by the enemy. One false move and he'll be arrested—or worse. All the while, he's carrying on a clandestine love affair.

But there is something about Lili Sanjari that Mayr doesn't know.

And global events are underway that will change his life in Tehran in ways he can't imagine.

6

Casablanca, Morocco

— JANUARY 24, 1943 —

The press conference was a complete surprise.

Yet here they all are, in the gardens of the luxurious Anfa Hotel, just outside the Moroccan city of Casablanca: a few dozen reporters, representing the world's wire services, newspapers, and military press agencies. Some are seated on folding chairs; others kneel on the grass.

The garden setting is deceptive, considering what lies just outside the hotel grounds. "The entire area for blocks around was full of troops, antiaircraft equipment and barbed wire," the *New York Times* explained. For the past ten days, the Anfa Hotel has hosted a conference between the American and British heads of state and their accompanying staff. Everything about the summit has been a closely guarded secret. Only now, with the proceedings over, can the participants reveal what has just transpired.

Facing the reporters, two of the leaders of the Allied war effort sit side by side in white leather armchairs: President Franklin Delano Roosevelt and Prime Minister Winston Churchill. The President and the Prime Minister know that

Winston Churchill and Franklin Roosevelt (*seated, left*) address reporters at the conclusion of the Casablanca summit. (Library of Congress)

the world is watching. They must appear completely united.

"These conferences have discussed, I think for the first time in history, the whole global picture," Roosevelt tells the gathered correspondents. "It isn't just one front, just one ocean, or one continent—it is literally the whole world; and that is why the Prime Minister and I feel that the conference is unique in the fact that it has this global aspect."

Nodding toward Churchill sitting next to him, the President continues. "I think we have all had it in our hearts and our heads before, but I don't think that it has ever been put down on paper by the Prime Minister and myself, and that is the determination that peace can come to the world only by the total elimination of German and Japanese war power."

Looking down at his prepared remarks, Roosevelt further clarifies the last point. "The elimination of German, Japanese, and Italian war power means the unconditional surrender by Germany, Italy, and Japan."

These words—"unconditional surrender"—cause a stir among the reporters. They look at the President in surprise, then their pens scribble furiously. Unconditional surrender means that the Allies will refuse to negotiate peace terms with Axis powers, Germany, Italy, or Japan. There will be

U. S. BOMBS GERMANY

Full Coverage *Of Roosevelt's Trip* See Pages 1, 2, 3, 5, 9, 14

DETROIT EVENING TIMES

RED LINE

Only Detroit Newspaper Carrying Both International News Service and United Press

43RD YEAR, NO. 120 DETROIT, MICHIGAN, THURSDAY, JANUARY 28, 1943 28 PAGES THREE CENTS

Roosevelt-Churchill Terms:

UNCONDITIONAL SURRENDER

U. S. Bombers In First Raid On Germany

LONDON, Jan. 27 (UP).—American heavy bombers made a large-scale attack today on the German naval base of Wilhelmshaven, a United States Army Air Force communique said.

The Wilhelmshaven raid was made by Flying Fortresses, the communique said. At the same time Liberator bombers attacked other targets in Northwestern Germany. Three American bombers are missing.

The American bombers, which were unescorted, destroyed a number of enemy fighters, the communique said.

LONDON, Jan. 27 (UP).—American bombs from American planes crashed on German soil today for the first time in this war, carrying into action the promise of President Roosevelt and Prime Minister Churchill to batter the Axis into unconditional surrender.

The raid was made against German naval installations and was a continuation of the 'round-the-clock assault of the Royal Air Force and the United States Army Air Force against German submarine bases and repair depots.

Flying Fortresses and Liberator bombers—big four-motored planes bristling with .50 caliber machine guns—made the attack.

The German Transocean News Agency broadcast from Berlin a report that British planes had raided Helgoland, an island 28 miles off the west German coast at noon today. Many four-engined bombers were shot down, the Germans claimed, by antiaircraft fire and fighter planes.

Whether the Germans mistook the American raiders for British is not known.

Several times in the last few weeks newspapermen have been told, "something big is coming off." But until today weather or other considerations always have prevented an extension of the United States daylight attacks to Germany proper.

The Weather

HOURLY TEMPERATURES

"That man Roosevelt sure does get around."

FORECAST For Detroit and vicinity: Not so cold tonight and tomorrow morning.

C. M. McARTHUR, DENTIST 1111 Griswold, over Kinsel's Hours: 9-5, Sundays 10-12—Adv.

Ed Flynn Wins Test In Senate

WASHINGTON, Jan. 27 (INS).—The Senate foreign relations committee today approved the nomination of Edward J. Flynn, New York political leader, to be minister to Australia.

The vote was 13 to 10.

The committee action was a victory for President Roosevelt but Flynn faces a bitter fight on the Senate floor against confirmation with debate scheduled to start next Monday. He must be confirmed by a majority vote.

Three Democratic members—George of Georgia, Van Nuys of Indiana and Gillette of Iowa—voted against confirmation while La Follette (P) of Wisconsin voted for Flynn.

Democratic leaders immediately predicted that the Senate will approve the Flynn nomination. Republicans, however, saw in the defection of three prominent Democratic members the possibility of a serious split in the Democratic Senate majority which would result in rejection of the nomination.

Yank Bombers Attack in Burma

NEW DELHI, Jan. 27 (UP).—American bombers raided Japanese installations at Rangoon and Mandalay and, with fighter escorts, attacked rail communications in Northern Burma, the 10th United States Air Force command announced today.

A communique said American planes scored hits in the Rangoon wharf area. Other bombers blasted rolling stock in the railroad yards at Mandalay.

Australian Dead: 6,826

CANBERRA, Jan. 27 (UP).—A representative of Premier John Curtin announced today that Australian battle casualties, since the war's beginning, were 6,826 killed, 23,892 missing, and 9,059 wounded.

THEIR DECISION: FIGHT TO TOTAL VICTORY

Photo by International News Sound Photos

MR. ROOSEVELT AND MR. CHURCHILL MEETING AT SEA IN '41 ...today they stressed unconditional surrender for the Axis...

Only 2,000 Japs On Guadalcanal

HONOLULU, Jan. 26 (UP) (delayed).—Reliable sources said today that probably fewer than 2,000 Japanese soldiers physically able to fight are left on Guadalcanal and that they control about 5 per cent of the island.

The recent seizure of Kolumbona village is believed to have definitely broken serious Japanese resistance.

2 Zeros Hit in Fight At Wake

WASHINGTON, Jan. 27 (UP).—American aircraft on a reconnaissance mission over Japanese-held Wake Island are believed to have shot down two of eight intercepting Zero fighters, the navy announced today. All of our planes returned safely.

The action occurred Monday and was the first reported over Wake since American airmen dumped 73,000 pounds of bombs on the island during the night of December 23-24.

Two Men Guilty In Beef Fraud

James Kelly and Earl Markhart, operating as the Royal Packing Company, 11542 East Jefferson avenue, today were found guilty by Traffic Judge Thomas F. Maher on charges of possessing 1,182 pounds of uninspected beef.

They also were found guilty of having diseased meat in their possession.

Whole Story Still Untold

From UP and INS Dispatches

WASHINGTON, Jan. 27.—The White House today revealed that the complete story of the African conference between President Roosevelt and Prime Minister Churchill has not been told and indicated that further momentous announcements will be made "as events unfold."

Presidential Secretary Stephen T. Early said that the announcements made by Mr. Roosevelt and the British leader following the historic meeting revealed only what can be told at the present time.

"Subsequent chapters undoubtedly will be written as events unfold," he added.

Washington's judgment coincided with London's that the President and Prime Minister had agreed on an early invasion of Europe where British and American troops will slug it out with Germany on the ground.

NOT WHOLE STORY

But the all-inclusive, global scope of the Casablanca communique and of the statements made by Mr. Roosevelt and Churchill at last Sunday's press conference suggest that some definite and satisfactory means must have been agreed upon to embrace China and Soviet Russia more firmly in the statement of policy.

Some of the newspapermen who covered the conference and reported it for American readers are beginning to evidence fears that they did not get all the story.

C. R. Cunningham of the United Press cabled last night that a "growing conviction" was evident among correspondents that much remained to be told.

NEWS TO COME

The London Daily Mail's G. Ward Price, a reporting veteran of World War I thought it over a couple of days and reported in a second dispatch today that only part of what happened at Casablanca had been revealed, that sensational news was to come.

The report of Walter Logan, United Press staff correspondent, that visitors arrived with Finnish tags on their baggage was to be considered. And rumors were rife.

A significant fact is that the

(Continued on Page Eight)

Map War Strategy At Session in Africa

CASABLANCA, Jan. 27 (INS).—An unwritten ultimatum calling for unconditional surrender or war to the last Nazi was served upon the Axis regimes of Germany, Japan and Italy today.

This, in brief, was the result of the most important war council in all history—the unprecedented meeting on Moroccan soil of President Roosevelt and Prime Minister Winston Churchill.

For 18 out of the 24 hours in each of 10 history-making days, the two great democratic leaders of a world plunged into war by Adolf Hitler's tyranny met with their military and political chiefs of staff in this sunny seaside city of the southern Mediterranean.

When they had finished, they had mapped a global war aimed at extinction of Axis military and political manpower and philosophy, brought together the divergent elements heretofore impeding consolidation of French resistance for liberation and paved the way for all-out offensive action against the enemy in every present and future theater of war.

Brushes Aside Precedent

Brushing aside precedent to become the first American President to fly the Atlantic, the first to leave his capital for foreign soil in time of war and the first also to set foot in an active combat zone, Mr. Roosevelt in his conference with Churchill achieved the following:

1—A definite, final and unalterable decision to fight the Axis with all the unified and co-ordinated strength of the United Nations until Hitler, Mussolini and Hirohito have been thrust to their knees in abject defeat.

2—An agreement between General Giraud, French high commissioner in North Africa, and Fighting French leader General De Gaulle for full military collaboration, insuring "total defeat of the enemy."

3—Completion of plans for maintenance of offensive action against the Axis in every arena of war, with all United Nations resources pooled to this end and all possible military aid given to Soviet Russia and China to insure continuation of the attrition which already has cut deep into the manpower and arms resources of the enemy.

Fourth War Consultation

Deeply tanned and in high spirits, and vastly encouraged by the fighting trim of American soldiers he reviewed and visited in the course of his 10-day stay in this outpost of United Nations power in Africa, President Roosevelt struck the entire leit-motif of this historic conference, which represented his fourth war consultation with Churchill.

The watchword and the slogan of the United Nations from this moment forward, he told correspondents, is "unconditional surrender."

He repeated it and emphasized it. He suggested

(Continued on Page Eight)

Bellamy Shot Echo

Police Complaint Charges Beautiful Madge, 39, of Assault With Deadly Weapon

SAN FRANCISCO, Jan. 27 (INS).—The "Frankie and Johnny" shooting episode on Nobb Hill last week, starring Madge Bellamy, star of stage and screen a decade or so ago, and A. Stanwood Murphy, wealthy lumber operator and socialite, took a more serious turn today.

The police department reversed itself and signed a complaint charging Miss Bellamy with assault with a deadly weapon on the person of Murphy—a felony.

Previously the police indicated strongly they were not much interested in the case, and so long as Murphy himself didn't appear anxious to be a complaining witness they were willing to let bygones be bygones.

But a few minutes before Miss Bellamy, once acclaimed by artists as the most beautiful woman in America, entered the court of Municipal Judge Clarence Morris to plead not guilty, Police Chief Charles Dullea announced that whether or not Murphy signed a complaint the police department would file one.

It was signed by Inspector Frank Lorry.

Partly dressed in black and wearing a short white ermine coat, Miss Bellamy, now around 39 and still very much of a beauty, was taken aback by the turn of events.

Murphy, who last New Year's Eve married the former June Almy, once a Paris model, was not in court but his attorney, Harold Faulkner, was.

In the Times TODAY

Japs Get Own Gas

Poison Fumes for Chinese Blown Back in Faces by Wind Shift; Also Bomb Selves

CHUNGKING, Jan. 27 (UP).—Japanese forces used poison gas against a Chinese unit January 6, but a shift in the wind blew the gas back in their own ranks and killed several hundred of their men, a Chinese communique said today.

The gas attack was made in the Linfen-Hungtung sector of southern Shansi Province, the communique said.

The same day, the communique said, five Japanese planes attempted to bomb Chinese positions but most of the enemy missiles fell on the Japanese ranks, killing an additional 100 men.

"The enemy lost more than 1,000 men that day," the communique reported.

DAVIES PREDICTS GAS

DENVER, Jan. 27 (INS).—Joseph E. Davies, former United States ambassador to Belgium and Russia, today predicted the German army this spring would resort to poison gas and possibly bacteriological weapons.

Davies also predicted that Germany would fail in its desperation attack; that first signs of the cracking of Nazi power would become evident, and that the United Nations will open several fronts during 1943.

The front page of the January 28, 1943, edition of the *Detroit Times* featuring the summit meeting of Prime Minister Winston Churchill and President Franklin D. Roosevelt of the United States in Casablanca, Morocco, where they agreed upon the need for unconditional surrender by the Axis powers. (*Chronicling America: Historic American Newspapers*, Library of Congress) no compromise to end the war, even if the enemy is willing to offer one. This means, for both sides, it's either total victory or total defeat.

The press are not the only ones surprised at Roosevelt's choice of words. Eyewitnesses notice Churchill's seemingly shocked reaction. The conference records show that "unconditional surrender" was discussed and agreed upon in the sessions, so Churchill wouldn't have been surprised that Roosevelt believed in such a policy. What does surprise him, though, is that Roosevelt has said these words in front of the world's press. Behind closed doors, there was no plan to go public, and Churchill later revealed that he probably would not have chosen to do so.

With Churchill looking on, Roosevelt continues, stating that this policy "does not mean the destruction of the population of Germany, Italy, or Japan, but it does mean the destruction of the philosophies in those countries which are based on conquest and the subjugation of other people." After a few more statements, he finishes.

Now it's Churchill's turn. In front of dozens of reporters, he has to decide whether to back up Roosevelt's language. "Well," he begins, "one thing I should like to say, and that is—I think I can say it with full confidence—nothing that may occur in this war will ever come between me and the President. He and I are in this as friends and partners, and we work together."

For Churchill, this personal solidarity with Roosevelt has always been clear. Within days of Pearl Harbor and Germany's declaration of war against the United States, the British Prime Minister boarded a royal battleship bound for Washington, DC, to formally establish a military alliance between the two nations.

Churchill was warmly received by the American press and public. On December 26, 1941, he became one of the few foreign leaders ever to address the US Congress. In his speech, he warned that "the forces ranged against us are enormous," but if the nations worked together, "the task which has been set us is not above our strength . . . its pangs and toils are not beyond our endurance."

The visit also provided an opportunity for the two leaders to get to know each other personally. Roosevelt liked to run a calm, orderly White House. Churchill's arrival was like a tornado. Upon arriving in the East Wing, he demanded a change of room and made elaborate requests for workspaces for his staff. He kept no regular schedule and often corralled his or the President's staff into spontaneous late-night meetings and policy sessions that would last until sunrise. His voice could be heard booming through the corridors.

One day in the late morning, when Roosevelt's aide Harry Hopkins wheeled him to Churchill's quarters to discuss a matter of policy that had come up, they were startled to walk in on the Prime Minister, as Hopkins described it, "stark naked and gleaming pink from his bath." To cut through the embarrassment, Churchill smiled and declared to his hosts that "the Prime Minister of the United Kingdom has nothing to hide from the President of the United States."

Despite their different temperaments, the two leaders formed an immediate friendship. Both were confident and optimistic men who worked extremely hard, valued camaraderie, and liked to mix laughter into their duties as head of state. Quickly dispensing with formalities, they spoke to each other frankly. Above all, what bonded them was a shared sense of duty: They would do anything and everything in their power to defeat Nazism and win the war.

Churchill's White House visit was planned to last for a week, but he extended it to over three weeks. By the end, Roosevelt and the White House staff were exhausted. Yet this first in-person meeting was only the beginning of their wartime partnership. Throughout 1942, the two leaders were in constant communication, and in public they always presented a united front. Now, almost one year later, here in Casablanca, Churchill's public and private friendship with Roosevelt is no doubt central in his mind as he speaks to the reporters gathered on the sun-dappled lawn of the Anfa Hotel.

The United States and the United Kingdom, Churchill states, will continue to prosecute the war with "unconquerable will." He pauses for a moment and then continues, "until we have procured the *unconditional surrender* of the criminal forces who plunged the world into storm and ruin." It's these two words—"unconditional surrender"—that will make headlines around the world. *Unconditional surrender* means that Nazi Germany and Imperial Japan cannot be negotiated with. They have already broken every promise, violated every treaty, and committed unthinkable war crimes. By repeating Roosevelt's phrase, Churchill is putting aside whatever reservations he may have had. They're in this together.

Despite its vastness and complexity, the global war at the start of 1943 can be roughly divided into three major theaters of operation. In the Pacific theater, the Japanese are fighting the United States, along with Australia and New Zealand, for control of the South Pacific region, encompassing dozens of countries and countless islands. On the Southern Front—which is sometimes called the Mediterranean or North African Front—British, American, and Canadian forces are battling with Italians and Germans for control over the Mediterranean region.

And then there's the Eastern Front between Germany and the Soviet Union.

No other arena of the war—or of any war, before or since—can compare to the apocalyptic destruction and mass suffering caused by Germany's offensive against the Soviet Union. The invasion was motivated partly by military strategy. Hitler believed that if his armies conquered the Soviet Union, then Nazi Germany would be unstoppable, and the war would be won.

But Operation Barbarossa was motivated by something more than just military strategy. According to racist Nazi ideology, Slavic people, which included Russians and Poles, were inferior—even subhuman—races. That meant, again according to the Nazis, that their lives were expendable. The Soviets were also Communists, whom Hitler despised. Communists had been the Nazi Party's political rivals in their fight to control Germany. Finally, the Soviet Union had a large population of Jewish people—the Nazis' so-called enemy whom they blamed for all their problems.

The result was an invasion of unimaginable brutality and horror. As Nazi armies razed towns and villages and slaughtered civilians, they intentionally also destroyed every farm, food supply, and irrigation system, unleashing a devastating famine across the countryside. The defending Soviet army faced their own brutal conditions. They were poorly fed, poorly equipped, and poorly trained. Medical treatment was so scarce that many injured soldiers were just left on the battlefield to die. Sometimes, Soviet military leaders sent badly armed infantry troops to almost certain death simply to slow down the enemy advance and buy some time for the defense. As a result, the Soviet casualty numbers were staggering. In Kyiv, over seven hundred thousand Soviet soldiers and civilians were killed or captured—and most of those who were taken prisoner later died in prisoner-of-war camps. Several other battles in 1941 and 1942 had casualties in the hundreds of thousands, and dozens of "smaller" battles had casualties of fifty thousand or more.

The German army also suffered brutal losses during the first two years of fighting in the Soviet Union, with a rough average of sixty thousand German casualties per month from the middle of 1941 to the end of 1942. By any normal standard of war, this is a massive number, but in comparison, the Soviets lost nearly ten times that number during the same period. And while the Axis losses came from soldiers dying in battle, the Soviet losses included huge numbers of innocent civilians.

Yet somehow, at the end of 1942, after eighteen months of devastation, the Soviet Union was still standing. Hitler had assumed that the Soviet Union would fall quickly. "We have only to kick in the door and the whole rotten edifice will come crashing down," he had predicted to his commanders. Nations like Norway, Belgium, Denmark, and even France had capitulated almost immediately after experiencing a taste of the Wehrmacht's fearsome power.

But the Soviet Union was not like Norway, Belgium, Denmark, or France. It was prepared to withstand the German army's most crushing blows, at almost any human cost, and keep fighting back. Over the long months of fighting, Soviet army officers gained more experience, and their troops became better trained. In addition, the United States was supplying them with an increasing flow of planes, trucks, weapons, food, and raw materials. And every month, thousands of Soviet teenagers reached the conscription age of seventeen and replaced those who had fallen in battle.

It was clear that a very long war still loomed ahead, one that would be measured in years, not in months. The only way for the Allied powers to end the catastrophe was to band together, come up with a unified plan, and fight with every ounce of strength they had. It would take complete solidarity among the Allied nations.

However, as Roosevelt was about to learn, solidarity, even in the face of such enormous devastation, wasn't nearly as easy as it seemed.

7

Tehran, Iran

— JANUARY 1943 —

Nazi spy Franz Mayr has a new mission.

Not *new,* exactly . . . but a *revived* mission, with a fresh sense of purpose.

The reason is a radio broadcast he has just heard. On the surface, the report was unremarkable: a routine news update from German-controlled Europe. But Mayr knows that it wasn't routine at all. The announcer spoke certain words and phrases in a manner that was intended for him and him alone.

The previous fall, Mayr heard that some Japanese diplomats would be allowed to visit Tehran. Through his connections, he was able to pass them a note, which he requested they bring back to Tokyo with them and then forward to Berlin. This note explained his circumstances and provided information about contacts in Turkey who could help him send messages safely. There was also a request for money and supplies, and Mayr provided map coordinates for a safe zone outside Tehran where German planes could drop parachutists and equipment. He also gave instructions for a specific repeated phrase to be included in a future radio broadcast, which would notify him that his spymasters back home had received his message.

The chances of this scheme working were so unlikely that when Mayr hears the broadcast using exactly the repeated phrase he suggested, it seems like nothing short of a miracle. What is more, it indicates that powerful people in Berlin not only still know who he is but are apparently willing to revive his mission. For the first time in nearly two years, Mayr no longer feels abandoned and alone. His grand vision of overthrowing Allied control and delivering Iran to the Nazis now seems attainable. Based on the radio broadcast he has just heard, help is on the way.

Mayr shares the incredible story of the coded radio

message with only a few of his closest allies in the city. Among them, of course, is his girlfriend, Lili Sanjari.

Remarkably, given the dangers and difficulties of Mayr's life as an undercover spy, the couple has been together for over two years now. In truth, though, Sanjari is more than Mayr's girlfriend. He has used her and her family connections to cultivate much of his underground network. And because she is local, and a native Farsi speaker, he often sends her to give messages to his Iranian contacts so he can keep his own identity and whereabouts a secret.

No doubt, there have been downsides. Just before the Allied occupation shut off Mayr's contact with Germany, he sent a formal request to Berlin that he be allowed to marry Sanjari. As a member of the Nazi Party, he was obliged to get permission to wed anyone who was not German and white. His superiors turn down his request. Sanjari is a native Iranian and therefore not suitable. The answer from Berlin disappoints the young couple. And, at some point in late 1942, perhaps out of frustration at Mayr's inability to marry her, or for other reasons of her own, Sanjari strays.

An avid pianist, she begins frequenting a nightclub that features a Western-style brass dance band. There, she meets and begins a relationship with a musician in the band, an American GI named Robert Merrick.

Needless to say, her Nazi boyfriend has no idea.

And, just as there are some things that Mayr doesn't know about Sanjari, there are some things that Sanjari doesn't know about Robert Merrick.

In addition to playing in a band and working as a lowly army transport clerk, Merrick is also an informant for the US Counter Intelligence Corps (CIC)—the army's intelligence division in Tehran.

So when Sanjari begins confiding to Merrick about her years-long relationship with Nazi spy Franz Mayr, Merrick conveys everything to his CIC contacts, who share the information with British intelligence in Tehran.

The British, who are closely monitoring Nazi activity in the region, tell the Americans to get Merrick to continue the relationship so they can learn as much as possible about Franz Mayr. And that's exactly what Merrick does.

Unfortunately for Mayr, he confides nearly every detail of his work to Sanjari. She knows where he's stayed, what secret aliases he's used, and, perhaps most importantly, the identities of the key players in the elaborate network of Nazi supporters he's worked so hard to cultivate.

In short, she knows almost everything about Mayr's Nazi operation.

That means that Robert Merrick knows almost everything, too.

And whatever Merrick knows, so, too, does the head of British intelligence in Tehran.

But what none of them knows, or could possibly know, is that in mere months, the world's attention will be on Tehran.

So, for Franz Mayr, 1943 is about to be a very interesting year.

8

Washington, DC

— JANUARY 30, 1943 —

It was "the most unprecedented and momentous meeting of the century."

So declare the front pages of American newspapers in the wake of the Casablanca conference. Naturally, the intricate war planning that occurred there remains mostly secret, but the elaborate public theater of the summit is a media sensation.

As Roosevelt arrives back on American shores, he has every reason to feel that the conference was a success. Still, no matter how much praise he receives, there's one aspect of the summit that remains, in his mind, a failure—or at least a serious disappointment. Stalin wasn't there. The country that has been doing most of the fighting against Nazi Germany—the Soviet Union—wasn't represented.

As Roosevelt saw it, the United States had an essential role to play in managing the Soviet relationship within the Allied alliance. The UK's relationship with the Soviets had been stormy since even before the war. Sure, after Hitler invaded the Soviet Union, Churchill publicly supported Stalin, but the long decades of distrust were not easy to overcome.

The problem was, forging an alliance with the Soviet Union was a complicated business. For starters, the Soviet Union was a Communist country, and to ally with the Soviet regime meant overcoming vast differences in politics, economics, and moral outlook. In a speech to Parliament, Churchill made clear, however, that this was precisely what the UK intended to do:

> No one has been a more consistent opponent of Communism than I have for the last twenty-five years. I will unsay no word that I have spoken about it. But all this fades

> away before the spectacle which is now unfolding . . . Any man or state who fights on against Nazism will have our aid . . . It follows, therefore, that we shall give whatever help we can to Russia and to the Russian people.

By allying with the Soviet Union, Churchill had to personally have dealings with the man who controlled the country with an iron fist: Joseph Stalin. Unlike previous Communist leaders, who were motivated at least in part by economic justice, Stalin had proven himself to be an authoritarian despot motivated only by raw power. His nickname, "The Man of Steel," arose from his personal ruthlessness. Like Hitler, Stalin routinely used murder and violence to eliminate political rivals. Like Hitler, Stalin committed mass atrocities against minority groups in his own country.

Roosevelt believed he had to take the lead. "I know you will not mind my being brutally frank," he wrote to Churchill in March 1942, "when I tell you that I think that I can personally handle Stalin better than either your

Foreign Office or my State Department. Stalin hates the guts of all your top people. He thinks he likes me better, and I hope he will continue to do so."

In May 1942, Roosevelt invited the Soviet Foreign Minister, Vyacheslav Molotov, to the White House to meet in person and plan strategy. The staff used the alias "Mr. Brown" for Molotov so the trip could be kept a secret until he returned to Moscow. Stalin appreciated the diplomacy—and the American military supplies.

But there was something else Stalin wanted, even more than planes and weapons. He wanted his two allies to launch a joint attack against Hitler's armies from the west, preferably directly across the English Channel into occupied France. Stalin believed that this strategy, and this strategy alone, would force Hitler to redirect enough of his armies away from the Eastern Front to give the Soviets a chance of seizing the advantage over the Wehrmacht and pushing them back into Germany.

For this reason, Stalin was deeply disappointed when, in early 1942, his Allied partners made clear that they would not launch any such "cross-Channel attack" for the rest of the calendar year. Some American military leaders had pushed for such a plan, but Churchill was unwilling to embark upon anything so risky. Simply put, he believed that the British and American forces weren't ready for the task. The German defense in Western Europe was simply too strong. Instead, throughout the summer and fall of 1942, the British and Americans engaged with Axis troops along the southern Mediterranean.

Stalin's frustration with their decision created a rift in the partnership. In his view, it was the Soviets who were doing most of the fighting and dying against Hitler's armies. As winter approached, he grew increasingly impatient.

Roosevelt knew this. In late 1942, when he and Churchill first came up with the idea of the Casablanca conference, his vision was that all three leaders would take part, making it easier to come to terms on key strategic concerns. Also, Roosevelt had never met Stalin in person, and he wanted to forge a personal working relationship with him.

However, over a series of letters between the two leaders in early December 1942, it became clear that Stalin's military responsibilities made it impossible for him to leave Russia at that time, much as he agreed it would be to everyone's advantage to meet in person. Roosevelt and Churchill had no choice but to proceed without him.

If Roosevelt can bring the Big Three face-to-face, he

believes, they can work through their differences, agree upon a military and political strategy, and present to the world a united front against Nazi Germany and the other Axis powers. Together, they can put an end to the unspeakable horrors of this global war.

It's an audacious idea—one that requires secrecy and new levels of security. If something goes wrong, it will be catastrophic.

9

TWENTY YEARS EARLIER . . .

Germany

In its early days, the Nazi Party, already a forceful and violent political organization, decided that it needed its own security force. The result was the Schutzstaffel (SS). Its members became a familiar sight at Nazi events, with their black uniforms, leather jackboots, and swastika armbands.

As the Nazi Party rose to power, the SS rose with it, ballooning in size from 280 men in 1929 to 52,000 in 1933. Soon, the SS also had its own police department (the Gestapo), a paramilitary force (the Waffen-SS), and the SD, or the Sicherheitsdienst, its dedicated intelligence service,

Reinhard Heydrich.
(National Archives)

through which it spied on its political enemies and monitored dissenters within its own ranks.

The SD was built from scratch by Reinhard Heydrich, a ruthless and arrogant Nazi who excelled at the backstabbing politics of the Reich. Heydrich created dossiers on his colleagues and their families so he had leverage over everyone, including his superiors.

Both Hitler and the SS leader, Heinrich Himmler, approved of Heydrich's relentless ambition. In 1934, Himmler handed him control of the Gestapo, the much-feared SS secret police. After that, Heydrich was elevated to be chief of the Reich Security Main Office, an umbrella organization that controlled all the SS security forces.

After an in-person meeting with Heydrich, a young SD recruit named Walter Schellenberg said, "I walked out of his office overwhelmed by the strength of his personality to an extent that I have never experienced before or since."

Not surprisingly for someone able to accumulate so much power within the Reich, Heydrich was a fervent believer in the nastiest elements of Nazi ideology. He was an avowed white supremacist who believed that all nonwhite peoples were biologically and culturally deficient. A lifelong antisemite, he referred to Jewish people as "the eternal subhumans." Like Hitler, he attributed Germany's struggles to the presence of Jews in the country and throughout Europe, and he believed that the vast apparatus of the SS—of which his SD and Gestapo were components—should be the "the offensive force which could initiate the final battle against the Jews."

Almost immediately after coming to power, Heydrich initiated that battle, using his immense powers to institute a reign of terror against the Jewish people of Germany. Heydrich's SS could arrest Jews, deport Jews, imprison Jews, interrogate Jews, attack and assault Jews, and, eventually, kill Jews. "Untouched by any pangs of conscience and assisted by an ice-cold intellect, he could carry injustice to the point of extreme cruelty," Schellenberg remembered.

It was Heydrich who came up with the concept of the Einsatzgruppen (operation groups). After the Wehrmacht defeated a town or a city, an Einsatzgruppe unit would follow the army and secure the newly occupied territory. What "securing" meant was rounding up and then arresting or murdering any civilians considered "enemies of the Reich."

For example, when Germany invaded Poland in 1939, Heydrich's SD created a list of sixty thousand Polish citizens considered a "danger" to the Reich, including any known or suspected Communists, professors, partisans, or Polish nationalists. In particular, they targeted Jewish people. Furnished with these lists, Einsatzgruppe units would track down these "enemies" and arrest them or shoot them on sight.

When the Germans invaded the Soviet Union, the work of the Einsatzgruppen only expanded. In Romania, Lithuania, Latvia, and Belarus, they enlisted local antisemitic or anti-Communist organizations to carry out the massacres of Jews, Roma, suspected Communists, and others. But mostly they acted alone.

In the villages, the Einsatzgruppen rounded up

civilians, brought them to the town square, and shot them. For larger towns and cities, the process was more complicated. They would corral together all the civilians identified as enemies. These people were often poor, didn't speak German, and didn't understand the fate that awaited them. The SS soldiers would force the people to hand over all personal belongings. Then they would march them a few miles outside the town, usually to an open field or a clearing in a forest, where a mass grave had already been dug. There, the soldiers would shoot the civilians, one by one, and throw their bodies into the grave.

As the war continued, the difficulty the Einsatzgruppen faced was that they couldn't kill people fast enough. Massacres required soldiers, weapons, and ammunition—all precious resources. In addition, Nazi commanders were seeing the negative effect on soldiers who carried out mass executions of innocent civilian men, women, and children. While many SS members had no problem doing the killing, and even relished it, some reported having nightmares and experiencing distress, especially those tasked with killing young children.

To address this problem, Heydrich and other SS leaders experimented with new methods. In the summer of 1941, Einsatzgruppen started using "gas vans." Soldiers would pack hundreds of victims into the cargo bays of diesel trucks, specially designed so the exhaust fumes from the engine would be directed into the back. By the time the truck arrived at a pre-dug mass grave, the passengers had been suffocated by the poisonous fumes and were dead.

But even these more efficient gas vans weren't able to handle the sheer numbers of people the SS wanted to eliminate. In the first two years of the war, SS death squads murdered several hundred thousand Jewish civilians in Eastern Europe and the Soviet Union. For the Nazis, it was not enough. It was a small fraction of the total Jewish population of the region. The conquered territories were too vast, the villages too many, and the SS soldiers, trucks, and rifles too few to deal with the number of Jewish people spread across Eastern Europe.

So SS leaders decided that they needed a new strategy to solve the "Jewish problem." About six months after the German invasion of Russia, Reinhard Heydrich invited key Nazi leaders to a conference in Wannsee, a leafy suburb southwest of Berlin. The goal of the conference, held in an ornate meeting room on January 20, 1942, was to formalize a "total solution to the Jewish question."

In his opening presentation, Heydrich outlined in dry bureaucratic language a program by which every Jewish population in Europe would be first exploited as slave labor and then murdered:

> In the course of the final solution the Jews are to be allocated for appropriate labor in the East. Able-bodied Jews, separated according to sex, will be taken in large work columns to these areas for work on roads, in the course of which action doubtless a large portion will be eliminated by natural causes. The possible final remnant will, since it will undoubtedly consist of the most resistant portion, have to be treated accordingly, because it is the product of natural selection and would, if released, act as the seed of a new Jewish revival.

In other words, the Nazis would work the Jews to death, and any who survived would be killed by other means.

Among the fifteen in attendance was Adolf Eichmann, head of the "Jewish Affairs" department of the Reich

Security Main Office. In advance of the meeting, Heydrich asked Eichmann to calculate the Jewish population in every European nation, including current and former Soviet territories. Eichmann prepared a breakdown of population numbers and shared the document with the group at the conference. His calculations showed that there were roughly eleven million Jewish people in Europe. With these figures, Nazi planners could formulate a strategy for rounding up, securing, and transporting all Jewish populations to labor camps where they could be either worked to death or killed by other means. *This* was the Final Solution: to murder eleven million Jewish men, women, and children.

What is notable about the Wannsee Conference is that not a single attendee raised the slightest objection to the program. There was no debate; they all went along with it. It's possible that they all knew already that Nazi forces were massacring Jewish populations in large numbers. Even so, the implementation of genocide as official government policy was a new idea—and no one objected.

As the conference adjourned, the attendees mingled and chatted. Heydrich took a seat in front of the room's elegant fireplace and allowed himself a moment of relaxation. In the following days, weeks, and months, he would throw himself into the planning of the Final Solution.

Land	Zahl
A. Altreich	131.800
Ostmark	43.700
Ostgebiete	420.000
Generalgouvernement	2.284.000
Bialystok	400.000
Protektorat Böhmen und Mähren	74.200
Estland - judenfrei -	
Lettland	3.500
Litauen	34.000
Belgien	43.000
Dänemark	5.600
Frankreich / Besetztes Gebiet	165.000
Unbesetztes Gebiet	700.000
Griechenland	69.600
Niederlande	160.800
Norwegen	1.300
B. Bulgarien	48.000
England	330.000
Finnland	2.300
Irland	4.000
Italien einschl. Sardinien	58.000
Albanien	200
Kroatien	40.000
Portugal	3.000
Rumänien einschl. Bessarabien	342.000
Schweden	8.000
Schweiz	18.000
Serbien	10.000
Slowakei	88.000
Spanien	6.000
Türkei (europ. Teil)	55.500
Ungarn	742.800
UdSSR	5.000.000
Ukraine 2.994.684	
Weißrußland aus-schl. Bialystok 446.484	
Zusammen: über	11.000.000

Adolf Eichmann's list estimating the total Jewish population of Europe by country or territory. (Political Archive of the Federal Foreign Office, RZ 214/100857)

Under his leadership, and that of Eichmann and others, dozens of SS "prison camps" and "labor camps" throughout Poland and Eastern Europe—places already filled with unspeakable suffering—would evolve into something else: genocidal "death camps."

Heydrich's own days were numbered. A few months later, in May 1942, while he was traveling in an open convertible through the city of Prague, two Czech resistance fighters jumped in front of the vehicle, guns raised.

It was an extraordinary assassination plot. The gunmen had parachuted into Prague from a plane flown from England by the Royal Air Force, and British intelligence helped them piece together Heydrich's car route so they could strike at the right time and place.

The gunmen didn't get a shot off, but one of them was able to toss a bomb at the car, which exploded on impact, severely wounding Heydrich. He died a few days later in the hospital. Hitler was furious that Heydrich had exposed himself to danger by driving in an open car, fuming:

> Since it is opportunity which makes not only the thief but also the assassin, such heroic gestures as driving in an open, unarmoured

> vehicle or walking about the streets unguarded are just damned stupidity, which serves the Fatherland not one whit. That a man as irreplaceable as Heydrich should expose himself to unnecessary danger, I can only condemn as stupid and idiotic.

If Hitler was angry at Heydrich's carelessness, he was absolutely enraged at the enemies of the Reich who had eliminated such an invaluable asset. He insisted on revenge. The SS tracked down the assassins, who were hiding in a church in Prague, but the two men killed themselves before they could be captured. That wasn't enough for Hitler, who demanded retribution. When German intelligence suggested that the assassins had links to the villages of Lezaky and Lidice, the Nazis had their targets.

SS units completely razed the tiny village of Lezaky, slaughtering everyone who lived there. In Lidice, they rounded up and killed all males over the age of sixteen—a total of 199 people—and put Lidice's women and children on trains to death camps in Poland.

The intelligence turned out to be false: There was no link between the assassins and those villages. But that hardly mattered to Nazi leaders. Their goal was to show the world how anyone who dared strike at the regime would be treated.

Heydrich's assassination didn't impede the Nazi genocidal program, though it did shake up the SS bureaucracy. Among the ripple effects, it advanced the career of his young protégé, Walter Schellenberg, who became the new head of Nazi foreign intelligence.

At the time, Schellenberg had no idea of how the dominoes of history would fall—or how, a year later, his newest mission would intersect with heads of state Joseph Stalin, Winston Churchill, and Franklin Delano Roosevelt. What he did know for sure, however, was what his mentor Heydrich taught him: that an SS leader must be willing to do anything—absolutely anything—to serve his Führer.

Walter Schellenberg. (Sueddeutsche Zeitung Photo/Alamy Stock Photo)

10

Fort Benning, Georgia

— APRIL 15, 1943 —

It's no ordinary train.

It's called the Ferdinand Magellan, and for the past few years it has had one purpose: to transport the President of the United States across the country. Referred to in government circles as "US Car No. 1," the Magellan has a half-inch-thick nickel-and-steel protective armor that encases all four sides as well as its roof. It also has bulletproof windows and two escape hatches through which the President and his wheelchair can be moved in case of emergency.

Most of the stops on this two-week cross-country tour

will be at military training facilities where the President will meet officers and observe troops. He'll also make several visits to factories producing warplanes, weapons, and other military supplies. The trip is about raising morale, generating headlines, and improving wartime public relations. For that reason, Roosevelt will give speeches, attend receptions, and greet saluting soldiers and cheering crowds.

While there may be plenty of cheering going on *outside* the train, inside there's a President who is dead serious. He's just received intelligence, via a decrypt of a radio transmission from Japan, that Admiral Isoroku Yamamoto, the Commander in Chief of the Japanese navy and the mastermind behind the attack on Pearl Harbor, is scheduled to fly on April 18 from Papua New Guinea to the Solomon Islands as part of his own inspection tour of Japanese troops and installations in the region.

What makes this intelligence so remarkable? For one thing, Yamamoto almost never leaves the safety of his command center aboard the Japanese navy's closely guarded battleship, the *Musashi*. Second, his means of air travel will leave him unusually exposed. A well-planned strike could take his plane down.

The Japanese obviously planned Yamamoto's trip with the absolute confidence that the Americans could not possibly learn about it. But US naval intelligence *did* learn about it. After intercepting the Japanese navy's radio transmissions, they successfully cracked the supposedly unbreakable Japanese code and deciphered the Admiral's itinerary.

President Roosevelt now has an opportunity to assassinate Admiral Yamamoto. He may never get the chance again. At this point in time, over a million US troops are fighting a savage war in the Pacific theater. Any advantage the United States can gain might bring victory a little closer and thereby save thousands of Allied lives. The US naval commanders have confirmed that the intelligence about Admiral Yamamoto is reliable. They're also sure that the strike is doable. If Roosevelt wants to take out the Admiral, he has the capability.

The question is: *Should* he?

A year ago, in the early spring of 1942, Roosevelt faced a similar decision. A series of Japanese victories had followed Pearl Harbor, and American morale was low. Military leaders proposed a daring idea. Medium-range B-25 bombers launched from an aircraft carrier right outside Japanese control could make it all the way to Japan, drop bombs over Tokyo, and have just enough fuel to reach Chinese airfields over the border.

No bombing raid over so huge a distance had ever been attempted before, and US military chiefs believed that Japan would be caught completely off guard. The raid would accomplish very little militarily, but the symbolism of American bombs falling on Japan's capital city would be a major morale boost at home.

Roosevelt gave the go-ahead, and the result was the famed "Doolittle Raid," led by celebrated aviator and US Army Air Force pilot Lieutenant Colonel Jimmy Doolittle. A total of sixteen B-25s with five-person crews flew over 800 miles undetected before crossing into Japan. They bombed some planned targets over Tokyo—mostly industrial and military installations—then headed for China.

The planes made it out of Japan unharmed but ran out of fuel before they could reach the Chinese airfields. One plane diverted to Russia, while the crews of the other fifteen parachuted into Chinese territory before their planes crashed. Some died in the drops or were captured by roaming Japanese troops on the ground, but the majority made it to the safety of Chinese villages, where they were sheltered and fed before returning home.

Just as Roosevelt had hoped, the raid generated jubilant headlines. Those who made it home were lavished with parades and medal ceremonies—instant war heroes. Jimmy Doolittle himself was awarded the Medal of Honor. The raid did negligible damage to Tokyo, but at a low point in the war it was a morale boost for Americans, putting a dent in Japan's aura of invincibility.

There was, however, a terrible price to be paid.

As expected, Japan was humiliated. Because they were already fighting US troops throughout the Pacific islands, there was little more they could do against the Americans that they were not already doing. But they *were* able to make a show of retaliation against someone else: the Chinese, whose airfields the Americans had used for the raids and whose civilians had given aid to the American pilots who crash-landed.

Japanese forces swept into China's undefended coastal provinces where the Americans had been helped. What happened next was a bloodbath. They raided dozens of towns, villages, and cities. "They shot any man, woman, child, cow, hog, or just about anything that moved," one Catholic missionary who was living in the town of Ihwang recorded in his diary. They also destroyed every hospital in the region and then poisoned the water supply, causing massive outbreaks of cholera, malaria, and dysentery with no medical facilities to treat the sick. In total, the Japanese retaliation murdered an estimated 200,000 to 250,000 defenseless Chinese civilians.

Sure, the Doolittle Raid gave Americans something to cheer about, but was a boost in morale worth the sacrifice of more than 200,000 innocent lives? That was the question Roosevelt faced when Chinese leader General Chiang Kai-shek wrote to him shortly after the events. Citing the deaths, Chiang told Roosevelt, "These Japanese troops slaughtered every man, woman and child in those areas. Let me repeat—these Japanese troops slaughtered every man, woman and child in those areas."

It is entirely possible that ordering a strike on Admiral Yamamoto's plane might lead to similar consequences. And there are other concerns that Roosevelt must weigh. For one, a strike against Yamamoto will alert the Japanese to the fact that the United States has been intercepting and decrypting its secret communications. The Japanese would be forced to change their codes and implement a new system. Should the United States yield an ongoing intelligence advantage just to take down one senior officer? Finally, there's the question of morality. Should a country that considers itself a beacon of democracy really be in the grim business of murdering enemy leaders?

The fact is that assassination is already part of the arsenal of the war—on both sides of the conflict. That the entire course of the war could be changed with a single bomb or bullet made assassination an irresistible tool.

To this day, there's no definitive record of how Roosevelt processed the information he received about Yamamoto. Nor is there a clear record of who he discussed it with or how the final order was given. There is only the order he gave.

"Get Yamamoto."

11

Berlin, Germany

— MARCH 1943 —

In early 1943, Walter Schellenberg, now head of Nazi foreign intelligence, learns that his organization sent two agents to Iran at the start of the war. After the British and Soviets occupied Iran, in August 1941, SD officials assumed that the two agents had been either captured or killed. With so many other pressing matters to attend to, the agency simply gave up on them and made no further effort on their behalf.

Then, just a few months ago, they received a "bolt from the blue": a message from Franz Mayr, one of the two agents. Miraculously, Mayr wasn't dead, and he had not been captured. Somehow, he'd survived the occupation. And not only had he survived, he'd established a robust underground network of German sympathizers and collaborators in the city of Tehran.

Mayr was requesting money, supplies, and wireless transmitters, and he provided coordinates for drop zones in the tribal regions outside Tehran where the Allies conducted little oversight. Consistent with his original mission, Mayr wanted to foster dissent against the Allied occupiers and make Iran ripe for a Nazi takeover.

But Schellenberg has something else in mind. Sabotage.

On the Eastern Front, Nazi forces are engaged in massive operations in southern Russia, close to the Iranian border, and Soviet forces are receiving supplies from the United States and Britain via the railroad that runs through Iran from the Persian Gulf. Mayr's surprise message has given Schellenberg one of the best things anyone can hope to find in a fight: an opportunity. With Mayr's network already in place, Berlin can airdrop weapons, explosives, and trained men to destroy or at least disrupt the railroad line used to deliver arms to the Soviets.

And so a new mission is born. They name it "Operation Franz," after Mayr himself, the intrepid spy who was left for dead only to reemerge two years later. If Operation

Franz succeeds, Nazi forces on the Eastern Front will gain an advantage over the Red Army, perhaps even a decisive one.

Schellenberg could use a victory. Both his intelligence organization and its rival, the Abwehr, recently experienced a humiliating failure. Almost two months ago, when Roosevelt and Churchill held their press conference on the lawn of the Anfa Hotel in Casablanca, the world press ran enthusiastic stories about the US–British summit. The problem for Schellenberg was that the Nazi leadership was taken completely by surprise that the event had occurred in Morocco. German intelligence had failed to learn the exact dates or location of the conference in advance.

Not only had they failed, the failure was a particularly embarrassing one. While the Allies were planning the conference, German intelligence had intercepted secret communications between the Americans and the British containing the word "Casablanca," in relation to a proposed summit. The analysts completely misunderstood the meaning. Because *casa blanca* translates to "white house" in Spanish, the Germans concluded that the conference was to be held at the White House in Washington, DC. It was only when they saw the international news coverage at the end of the summit that they realized their mistake.

Hitler was furious at the error. Although Schellenberg's foreign intelligence office was not singled out for blame, the truth was that his organization had completely failed to predict the correct date or location.

Schellenberg is hoping that Operation Franz will win him the Führer's favor.

12

Iran

— APRIL 15, 1943 —

The weapons hit the ground with a thud. They're in a heavy, sealed crate that kicks up dirt and sand on impact.

The desert is quiet again under the moonless night sky until, several seconds later, there's another thud, a few dozen yards away. This time, it's not a crate but a human being that lands, followed by an open parachute.

Over the next several minutes, five other crates attached to five other parachutists hit the ground, one by one. If anyone was in the vicinity, they would hear voices calling out in German as the parachutists try to locate one another.

Eventually, the band of six takes stock. The landing seems to have been successful. All six men are uninjured, and most, if not all, of their gear is intact.

But then the men realize—perhaps immediately or perhaps by the first light of morning, after a few hours of sleep in their tents—that something is amiss. According to their compasses and the position of a nearby mountain range, they're not where they're supposed to be. Instead, they're several dozen miles south from where they intended to land, which puts them farther than they'd like from their destination: the city of Tehran.

What went wrong? The men aren't sure. The coordinates of the drop zone were sent to Berlin in a message from Franz Mayr, the spy in Tehran after whom their mission was named. He's the man they need to get to the city to find. Perhaps Mayr's maps were faulty, or maybe the pilot made an error. Whatever the reason, they must now adapt to the situation.

Five of the six paratroopers are young men, still in their twenties. The sixth, Karl Korel, is more experienced. At thirty-eight, he's the veteran, and, unlike the others, he's been to Iran before and can speak Farsi. Although he's not technically in charge of the mission—he was originally brought on as a translator—Korel quickly assumes a leadership role. It's up to him to get them out of this potentially dangerous situation, stuck in a desert in a hostile country.

After some deliberation, Korel determines that the full group of six shouldn't make the trek across the desert. There's too much to carry, and they'll run out of water. Instead, he'll cross the desert by himself, traveling light, while the others camp with the gear in the nearby foothills. If he can make it to Tehran and locate Mayr, he'll return with trucks or camels to retrieve everyone else. And if the authorities discover him and hand him to the British or the Soviets, well, then a terrible fate awaits him.

It's not an ideal plan, but they don't have many options. The rest of the group has no choice but to wait in the desert, try to conserve water, and hope for the best.

Their adventure is just beginning.

13

Washington, DC

— APRIL 29, 1943 —

When the Ferdinand Magellan pulls into Union Station in Washington, DC, after two full weeks on the road, one person is probably more relieved than anyone else.

He's the man who keeps the President safe. His name is Mike Reilly. As head of the White House Secret Service, he leads a team of agents who follow the President everywhere he goes. For Reilly, a long, cross-country journey with the President is an exercise in nonstop stress and anxiety. That's because, from Reilly's point of view, every stop, every speech, and every public appearance holds the potential for disaster.

Roosevelt and Reilly are an odd pair, to be sure, but they've formed an unusually tight bond. Roosevelt is a northeastern aristocrat who attended the finest schools and grew up with every privilege; Reilly is a brawny, working-class, former high school football player from Montana, who is, as he later described himself, "an Irishman who sometimes had more muscle than brain."

Mike Reilly (*left*) with FDR (*right*). (Bettmann/Getty Images)

Roosevelt's physical disability gives their relationship an added level of intimacy. At a time when little or nothing was done in public spaces to accommodate the needs of wheelchair users, Reilly is the one who makes sure there are ramps for Roosevelt's wheelchair and that the President's sleeping quarters and bathrooms are accommodating to his needs. Sometimes, the broad-shouldered Reilly has to carry the President up or down stairs or through spaces inaccessible to a wheelchair.

The most obvious concern for Reilly, like everyone in the Secret Service, is stopping those who intend to do the President harm. During wartime, the circle of potential enemies expands from the usual deranged individuals and domestic extremists to foreign enemy agents, saboteurs, and assassins. "Traditionally American Presidents are shot," Reilly wrote in his memoir, "but they could be bombed, poisoned, stabbed, or murdered in a train wreck. Our job was to prevent any of these."

It was Reilly who created a separate location for all incoming White House mail and packages so that a trained team could screen every parcel for bombs and explosives. It was Reilly who came up with a system to test for poison samples in food received as gifts from all over the world. And it was Reilly who, before the President flew to

Casablanca earlier in the year, traveled in advance to each one of the layover stops along the route and inspected every airfield, tarmac, car route, and hotel.

The responsibility of keeping this unusually vulnerable President safe gave Reilly "shivers in the daytime and nightmares in bed." So, on April 29, when the Ferdinand Magellan returns to Washington, DC, and the President safely makes his way back to the White House after a two-week journey around the country, including a brief stayover in Mexico, Mike Reilly is relieved.

What Reilly doesn't know is that Roosevelt spent much of that train journey anxiously awaiting top secret communications from his senior naval commanders. The subject? Operation Vengeance. The plan to kill Admiral Yamamoto. On April 18, a squadron of sixteen P-38 US fighter planes located and trailed two Japanese bombers escorted by nine fighters. Sure enough, Admiral Yamamoto was in one of the bombers, on his way to a scheduled tour of Bougainville Island in Papua New Guinea.

With the element of surprise on their side, the US planes moved on the squadron, dispatched the Japanese fighters, then circled in on their target. One of the P-38s swung behind Yamamoto's plane, and the American gunners unleashed a volley of bullets. The Admiral's bomber started

Admiral Isoroku Yamamoto (in white) gives what will be his final address to Japanese naval pilots. Targeted killings of high-ranking officials were common practice during World War II. (ullstein bild via Getty Images)

spewing black smoke, and the plane crashed into the jungle below. The next day, a Japanese search-and-rescue party found the crashed plane with Yamamoto's body nearby.

Unlike with the Doolittle Raid, this time US officials kept the Yamamoto strike under wraps. It was a clandestine operation, and they wanted to keep it that way. The Japanese also kept it a secret, knowing that the loss of the revered Admiral would cripple public morale in Japan. They waited a full month to announce Yamamoto's death and never revealed what they knew: that it was the result of a premeditated strike by the Americans, and that US intelligence had decrypted the Japanese navy's supposedly unbreakable codes. Japan's official statement, repeated in newspapers around the world on May 21, was simply that Yamamoto had "engaged in combat with the enemy and met gallant death."

Roosevelt's first public comments about it are at a White House press conference shortly after the Japanese announcement. Toward the end of the press briefing, a reporter asks him, "Would you care to comment on the death of the Japanese Admiral?"

"He's dead?" Roosevelt says, after a pause. "Gosh!"

While he makes out that he is learning about the incident for the first time, Roosevelt's tone is a nod and a wink to reporters that he knows more than he is letting on. If there's any smugness in his voice, it's because he is proud of what his military has accomplished. US naval intelligence decrypted a series of codes that the Japanese believed to be unbreakable, and as a result, one of Imperial Japan's most brilliant and respected military leaders, and the mastermind behind Pearl Harbor, has been permanently removed.

Still, Roosevelt can't rest easy. Nor can Mike Reilly. America's enemies are also capable of intercepting communications and breaking secret codes, and—as Roosevelt and his bodyguard Mike Reilly will soon learn—assassination plots can go both ways.

14

Tehran, Iran

— LATE APRIL 1943 —

Karl Korel needs a lucky break.

So far, the entire mission has been difficult. The parachute drop went off course. The trek across the desert was dangerous in itself. And now he is walking into Allied-occupied Tehran, alone, with no support, no protection, and no means of communication with either his team in the desert or his superiors in Berlin.

His goal, at this point, is near impossible: to locate, in this teeming city of three-quarters of a million people, a single man, the Nazi SD agent Franz Mayr. Not only is this already a tall order, but there is also another problem. Mayr is in hiding. He's probably wearing a disguise, almost certainly doesn't use his real name, and could be in a basement or back room anywhere in the sprawling metropolis.

However, in his quest to find Mayr, Korel has a few things going for him. Unlike everyone else on his team, he can speak and read some Farsi. He's been in Tehran before, back in 1941, before the Allies seized control. During that visit, he actually met Franz Mayr, as well as others in Mayr's circle.

It's this fact that will make the difference.

While Korel is wandering around downtown, probably somewhat aimlessly, looking for clues in cafés and markets, he happens to spot an older woman who looks familiar. It's a stroke of luck almost too good to be believed. As he gets closer, he confirms that it's the mother of Lili Sanjari, Franz Mayr's girlfriend.

Mayr was already in a relationship with Lili when Korel met him back in 1941, and Korel also met Lili's parents at that time. The question is, how safe is it to approach her mother? For all Korel knows, the Sanjari family could have switched loyalty to the Allied side when the British and Russians took control of the city. If so, this woman might lead him straight to the Allied authorities. Still, the task of finding Mayr in this city is otherwise so daunting that Korel probably feels he hasn't got much choice.

Amazingly, his luck holds. After he introduces himself, the woman agrees to help. She confirms that Mayr and her daughter are still a couple, and, even better, she knows Lili's whereabouts. This is how, on roughly April 15, 1943, Operation Franz connects with Franz Mayr. There is no record of where Lili's mother brings Korel, nor of what is said at his meeting with Mayr. Surely the two Nazi agents would have been brimming with questions for each other. But there wouldn't have been much time for discussion. Korel needs Mayr's help to gather camels and supplies for a return trip through the desert to get the other members of the mission, who have been camping out in the foothills for over a week now.

Based on how long it took Korel to reach the city, it'll take another full week to get back to his colleagues, and another week on top of that for the group and their supplies to return to Tehran. That's three weeks of back-to-back treks through the Iranian desert. And that's just to get the mission started. For now, though, Korel can take satisfaction that the first objective of Operation Franz has been completed. Thanks to his competence and a stroke of good luck, the mission has established contact with SD agent Franz Mayr.

For Mayr, it must be even more gratifying. For almost two years, he's been operating alone, in hiding, and fearing for his life, with no support from his home country. In spite of this, during that time, he never gave up his mission, convinced that Tehran is important to the Nazi war effort. Almost single-handedly, he's built and cultivated a network of Nazi sympathizers and supporters. Now, for the first time, he has the support he's craved. Soon, he'll have supplies, money, wireless radios, and new personnel to work with.

Yet at this moment, Mayr and his companions are still unaware of just how important this city will soon be on the global stage. Indeed, the Nazi mission in Tehran is about to change into something none of them can imagine.

He looks like an ordinary teenager on a bike.

At nineteen years of age, Gevork Vartanian is slender, with Eastern European features lightly tanned by the Iranian sun. He spends most of his days crossing the streets and back alleys of Tehran, sometimes with companions but often alone, occasionally stopping to peer into doorways or to say a few words to shopkeepers or regulars at the city's outdoor markets.

Bicycles are a common mode of transportation in Tehran, so Vartanian looks no different from the many ordinary residents who get from place to place on two wheels. But he is far from ordinary. Vartanian is an undercover Soviet agent.

Born in 1924 in southern Russia, Vartanian has spent most of his life in Tehran. He speaks fluent Farsi and knows the ins and outs of Iran's complicated capital city. By the age of sixteen, he is working for the NKVD, the Soviet intelligence service, in Tehran. He is one of a team of young recruits—mostly all still teenagers, and they all go by bike. Vartanian's superior jokingly called them the "Light Cavalry," and, as Vartanian would later recall, "This name stuck."

It's a clever idea. The cavalry can get around the city quickly and easily; they don't need expensive vehicles or gasoline; and, as bike-riding teenagers, they blend in and don't draw any attention to themselves. This makes them perfect spies. Their job is to seek out enemy activity in Tehran, specifically to monitor and identify fascist agents.

Soviet intelligence knows, of course, about a suspected Nazi spy operating in Tehran. They even know his name:

Franz Mayr. Through their counterparts in British intelligence, they've learned that this spy, working undercover and in hiding, has been building a powerful pro-Nazi network in the city. It's no secret that many Iranians resent the Allied occupation of their country. Some are still loyal to Reza Shah, the previous leader, who was friendly with Hitler.

The last thing the Allied authorities in Iran want is a pro-Nazi resistance movement to threaten Allied control of the region. For the Soviets in particular, the stability of Tehran is a matter of supreme importance. Just over the border, they're fighting for their very existence against the invading Nazi armies, sacrificing hundreds of thousands of lives every month. This extraordinary effort depends on the regular flow of American arms and supplies—a flow that goes straight through Iran.

On a typical day, Vartanian and his fellow Light Cavalry members cruise the city, checking in on informants, passing messages from their superiors to intelligence sources, monitoring suspected pro-Nazi dissidents, and generally looking out for anything unusual. Lately, there's been plenty. According to local reports, German planes have been spotted in the sky over the desert. There are rumors of enemy paratroopers outside the city—and now, possibly, within it.

The Light Cavalry better be ready.

15

Berlin, Germany

— LATE APRIL 1943 —

Walter Schellenberg carefully eyes the uniformed man who has just entered his office.

As a high-ranking intelligence officer, Schellenberg has many potential enemies and is always on alert for plots against him. "There were times when I felt more like a hunted beast than the head of a department," he later recalled.

To protect himself, he's taken special precautions. Microphones are hidden in the walls, under the desk, and even in one of the lamps, so that every conversation and every sound is automatically recorded.

But a microphone is no help if he is attacked. For that, he needs something more practical. "My desk was like a small fortress," Schellenberg wrote. "Two automatic guns were built into it which could spray the whole room with bullets. These guns pointed at the visitor and followed his or her progress toward my desk. All I had to do in an emergency was to press a button and both guns would fire simultaneously."

The man now sitting in front of Schellenberg's desk likely has no idea that two automatic guns are currently pointed at him. But even if he did, he would probably not be intimidated. He's someone who's used to facing danger. His name is Otto Skorzeny. At thirty-four, he's a veteran officer in the Waffen-SS with the equivalent of a lieutenant's rank. Because of an injury received on the Eastern Front, he can't serve on the front line for now, but Skorzeny has a particular set of skills—engineering, explosives, flight training, advanced weaponry, and leadership in battle—that make him extremely useful.

Schellenberg has summoned Skorzeny to his office to discuss operations in Iran. He has plans for another Iranian mission, soon to be called Operation Anton, that will parachute a team of agents armed with weapons and explosives into the northern tribal regions of the country. There, they

Otto Skorzeny.
(Shawshots/Alamy Stock Photo)

will link up with an Abwehr agent to sabotage train lines and other targets, provide weapons and money to local collaborators, and complement the Operation Franz mission.

The concept of special forces—small, mobile teams of specialized soldiers sent to fulfill discrete tasks—has recently gained currency in Nazi leadership circles. The vast German armies encountered stiff resistance from the Soviets on the Eastern Front, and the progress of the war has stalled. Using small, elite, and fast-moving teams to accomplish specialized and often secret missions is one way to take advantage of Germany's superior technology and training. Nazi leaders hope they'll tip the balance of power in their favor.

Schellenberg knows he needs someone to recruit and train agents for these elite field operations. That's where Skorzeny comes in. Skorzeny is a physically powerful presence: six foot four and wide-shouldered. He has a fencing scar on his cheek from his teenage years—a source of pride among a certain set of German men. He speaks firmly and exudes confidence. Most importantly, he has the skills and knowledge for the job.

By the end of the interview, the two men have all but agreed on a plan. Skorzeny will take over and expand the SD's special operations training program. He will recruit soldiers and intelligence agents and train them in explosives, sabotage, and paramilitary operations. In recognition of this role, he will be promoted to Captain.

Throughout their conversation, the two Nazis have been pretending to get along while secretly sizing each other up. Skorzeny, who considers himself a soldier first and foremost, perceives the physically unimpressive Schellenberg as a bureaucrat and a man who isn't "as clever or clear-seeing as he thought he was." Schellenberg, meanwhile, doesn't have much patience for crude military men like Skorzeny. He considers himself a person of refined taste and intellect and prefers to do business with the social elite of the Nazi hierarchy.

Still, the arrangement is mutually beneficial, and they agree to work together. The guns underneath the desk will not be needed on this occasion.

Yet what neither man realizes is that because of their short meeting today, soon-to-be-Captain Otto Skorzeny—previously a midlevel Waffen-SS officer little known outside his division—is on his way to being known all over the world as the "Most Dangerous Man in Europe."

16

Washington, DC

— MAY 5, 1943 —

It's just a letter.

It's typewritten, single-spaced, just a few paragraphs in length. And it's addressed to Joseph Stalin.

President Roosevelt composed it himself. He believes that it could alter the alliance for the better and help win the war. It is so important and so confidential that he trusts one person and one person only to carry it across the world and deliver it by hand.

The chosen messenger, Joseph E. Davies, now sits in the Oval Office, in front of the President's desk. From 1936 to 1938, Davies served as Roosevelt's Ambassador to the Soviet

Union, and he is one of the few people in Washington the President trusts to do business with Moscow. What's more, he knows that both Molotov and Stalin think favorably of Davies.

Davies now reads the letter. It begins:

> My Dear Mr. Stalin:
> I am sending this personal note to you by the hands of my old friend, Joseph E. Davies. It relates solely to one subject which I think it is easier for us to talk over through a mutual friend . . .
>
> I want to get away from the difficulties of large Staff conferences or the red tape of diplomatic conversations. Therefore, the simplest and most practical method that I can think of would be an informal and completely simple visit for a few days between you and me.

The letter continues: "It is my thought that neither of us would want to bring any Staff . . . and that you and I would talk very informally and get what we call 'a meeting of the minds.'" Roosevelt goes on to suggest a date: "You and I ought to meet this summer." As for location, he writes, "Africa is almost out of the question in Summer and Khartoum is British territory. Iceland I do not like because for both you and me it involves rather difficult flights and, in addition, would make it, quite frankly, difficult not to invite Prime Minister Churchill at the same time." He adds, "Therefore, I suggest that we could meet either on your side or my side of Bering Strait."

He means Alaska.

Now aware of the contents of the letter, Davies responds with two obvious questions: Why isn't Churchill invited, and does Churchill know that Roosevelt is planning this meeting without him? It's public knowledge that Roosevelt and Churchill have been pushing for a meeting of the Big Three.

"Three is a crowd, and we can arrange for the Big Three to get together thereafter," Roosevelt says somewhat cryptically. "Churchill will understand, I will take care of that."

In other words, Churchill does *not* know that Roosevelt is pursuing this meeting without him. What is more, Roosevelt is making sure that Churchill won't come, and he is doing so behind Churchill's back.

So why is Roosevelt deceiving his closest and most loyal

partner? The answer has to do with the single biggest decision the Allies must make in the entire war—the decision that could be the key to defeating Nazi Germany.

The cross-Channel attack.

Stalin has always been consistent on the issue. Since the beginning of the alliance, he's been adamant that his partners must open a "second front" against Germany by striking directly from the west. This and this alone, Stalin believes, will force Hitler to divert enough ground forces from the Eastern Front so the Soviet army can gain a decisive advantage and push the Nazi armies back.

At first, US military leaders were optimistic that such an assault could be launched soon after America's entry into the war. Shortly after Pearl Harbor, the US Joint Planning Staff presented a strategy for a combined American and British cross-Channel attack to take place in July or August of 1942. Although the idea was still under debate, President Roosevelt told Molotov to expect a "second front" in 1942—a message Molotov took home to Stalin.

The problem was that the British weren't on board yet, and the idea of diverting hundreds of thousands of Nazi troops away from Russia toward the beaches of northern France, just a few dozen miles from England's southern coast, meant something entirely different for them than for the Soviets or the Americans. The British planners also pointed out the many tactical and logistical difficulties of an amphibious landing in front of the most powerful army in the world, arguing that US troop numbers and arms production were not yet sufficient for such an operation.

Instead, in 1942, the Americans and the British embarked upon Operation Torch, a mission to push Italian and German forces out of North Africa and thereby gain control of Mediterranean ports and sea lanes. This was the beginning of the "Southern Front" that would be the main European theater of operations for American and British ground troops. The UK and the United States continued to support the Soviet army with an increasing flow of arms and supplies.

Their decision frustrated Stalin deeply. His armies and his country were facing annihilation, suffering millions of lives lost and enduring famines and massacres, while the Americans and the British were, to Stalin's mind, tinkering with sea lanes in a faraway region that was of minor consequence. They were not *really* confronting Nazi Germany. But Stalin didn't have much choice other than to go along with his allies' strategy. He desperately needed the arms and supplies that Roosevelt was sending.

And so the Russians continued enduring the Nazi onslaught largely on their own.

If the United States and the UK couldn't or wouldn't attempt a cross-Channel attack in 1942, then, Stalin assumed, surely 1943 would be the year in which they would. Until then, the Soviet Union would weather the Nazi storm. Its soldiers and civilians would continue to die in the millions, month after month, but at least the United States and Britain would join the fight the following spring or summer.

Roosevelt believed this, too. Throughout 1942, US and British war planners did try to come up with strategies to strike Western Europe from England in 1943. But they could never agree on the specifics or on the timing. With every proposed operation, someone would decide that it was too complex or too risky, the cost of failure too high.

A pattern emerged: The Americans would be ready to move forward with a cross-Channel attack, but then the British would come up with reasons to reject or delay the plan. Churchill especially became more and more attracted to the Mediterranean theater of war, where the Allies could achieve small but decisive victories. The Mediterranean, he believed, was the "soft underbelly" of Europe through which the Allies could safely advance. Although this strategy led to Allied victories in North Africa throughout 1942, it wasn't doing much to stop the cataclysm in Eastern Europe and the Soviet Union. Nor was it directly threatening Hitler's domination of Western Europe.

At the conclusion of the Casablanca conference in January 1943, Roosevelt and Churchill had still not resolved this critical issue of the second front. They made grand proclamations about the progress of the war in the Pacific and around the Mediterranean, but they couldn't agree on a plan for attacking across the Channel into northern France.

In the months after the conference, Churchill's constant negativity and wavering on the cross-Channel attack threatened to corrode the relationship. Roosevelt began to fear what was once unthinkable: that the Americans and the British would not be ready to execute a cross-Channel attack before the onset of winter and would once again have to postpone until the following spring.

It is in this context that Roosevelt goes behind Churchill's back and sets up his one-on-one meeting with Stalin. His goal is to establish a personal connection with the Soviet leader and to assure him that the United States is fully committed to supporting the Soviets in the war. They may have to delay the cross-Channel attack again, but, in the end, the Americans will come through on the issue of the second front, and Roosevelt will make sure that Churchill complies.

Roosevelt knows that Stalin has never fully trusted the British, and he fears that if the three of them meet in person and Churchill displays any hesitancy about attacking Hitler in France, Stalin may lose faith in the alliance. The results would be disastrous. Will Churchill be offended? Of course he'll be offended. But while Roosevelt is well aware that his personal loyalty to Churchill is important, it's not as important as defeating Hitler. And to defeat Hitler, the alliance with the Soviets must be solid.

To make matters more complicated, at this very moment, Churchill is on a ship bound for the United States, scheduled to arrive on May 11, a week after Roosevelt's meeting with Joseph Davies. Once again, Churchill gives a long address to both houses of Congress and once again he is received rapturously by his American audience. He speaks at length about the tight bond between the two nations and of his unity with Roosevelt. He also brings up the possibility of a Big Three conference. Referring to Roosevelt and himself, he declares, "We, both of us, earnestly hope that at no distant date we may be able to achieve what we have so long sought—namely, a meeting with Marshal Stalin."

As he speaks those words, Churchill has no idea of the machinations currently underway to cut him out of any such meeting.

17

Tehran, Iran

— MAY 1943 —

No one can say that Franz Mayr isn't ambitious.

Since being forced into hiding nearly two years ago, his goal has been nothing less than the overthrow of the pro-Allied government in Iran, with himself in the leading role. Given the arrival of personnel, weapons, wireless transmitters, and other supplies from Berlin via Operation Franz, surely his grand vision is close to being realized.

However, from the moment Karl Korel returns to Tehran with the other members of his team, all of whom survived their time camping in the desert, Mayr finds himself at odds with his new companions. For starters, he's annoyed to learn that they've called their mission "Operation Franz." Sure, it's a tribute to him, but he's a man in hiding in an enemy country. If any of the team is captured and interrogated by the Allies, or if documents are confiscated, the mission's name might be revealed—meaning that his name will also be revealed.

Even worse, Mayr learns that the goals of Operation Franz do not match his own. He has developed an underground resistance movement, ready to help overthrow Allied control when the Nazi armies make their move. The Operation Franz team, on the other hand, has been sent on an unrelated mission: to sabotage the Trans-Iranian Railway, with the goal of halting or slowing the flow of US arms to the Red Army in southern Russia. To Mayr's thinking, this is foolish. The railroad is well protected by British and Soviet security forces, and a handful of novice German saboteurs will most likely be caught and arrested—threatening Mayr's long-running operations in Tehran.

Neither does Mayr approve of the fact that the Operation Franz team brought a cache of explosives and heavy weapons into the city. These now need to be stored in safehouses and basements, and if the wrong eyes see them, the entire mission could fall apart, taking Mayr with them.

Franz Mayr (*standing, right*), with five of the six members of the Operation Franz team. Karl Korel, the oldest member of the team, is not pictured. (National Archives [U.K.], ref. KV2/1481)

Finally, Mayr is disappointed with the team itself. Other than Karl Korel, they're young and inexperienced. None of them knows anything about the region—and they know even less about espionage. A few of them are trained in explosives and sabotage, but that's not helpful to Mayr's goals, and they barely know how to operate the equipment they brought.

While Mayr has no choice other than to work with these fellow Germans, he's disappointed in the caliber of person the Berlin spymasters chose to send. The one exception is Karl Korel, who, of course, he met a few years earlier. Korel is mature and experienced, he speaks Farsi, and he knows his way around the city. The fact that Korel found Mayr at all is impressive. In Korel, Mayr believes he has a real partner.

Unfortunately, Korel is about to become his biggest problem.

Shortly after his return from the desert with the Operation Franz team, Karl Korel begins to look unwell. They all see it. He's feverish and exhausted, and experiencing terrible stomach pains. Soon he can barely move. His living conditions—hiding in the basements and attics of safehouses—don't help matters.

They can't just take Korel to a hospital. Doing so might alert the authorities to the team's presence in the city. And yet Korel clearly needs medical treatment. Finally, Mayr finds a doctor willing to visit Korel in secret. After assessing the patient, the doctor has bad news. Korel has typhoid fever, a life-threatening disease caught by eating food or drinking water containing the typhoid bacteria. Proper treatment requires antibiotics, which neither the doctor, nor anyone else in the group, has.

Korel's condition slowly worsens. At some point in mid-May, he's dead.

It is a devastating loss for Mayr and the Franz team. It also poses an immediate logistical problem. What do they do with Korel's body? For the same reason they couldn't take Korel to the hospital when he was ill, now they can't bring his remains to the city morgue. Nor can they get caught transporting a corpse through the streets of Tehran. Somehow, they need to get rid of the body, and it needs to be done quickly and discreetly.

They realize that they have no choice but to cut the body into pieces and take it out of the city in cases and rucksacks. Mayr enlists some local collaborators to do the dirty work. Then, in a moonlit field on the outskirts of Tehran, Mayr and the surviving members of Operation Franz give their comrade a proper German burial.

Korel's death and its grisly aftermath cast a shadow over the whole team. They've lost one of their more experienced members—the only one who could speak the local language. For Mayr in particular, Korel's death is a tough blow. In his mind, the other members of the group are mostly incompetent. They don't know how to conduct themselves as foreign agents, and they depend on Mayr for everything. Housing them, feeding them, and protecting them becomes an endless burden.

Still, not everything is a disaster. The parachutists brought wireless radio transmitters with them. After a few false starts, the team has been able to set them up and obtain a usable signal. Through trial and error, they figure out how to send and receive messages to and from the German embassy in Turkey, and sometimes directly to Berlin.

By the early summer of 1943, Operation Franz is in an uncertain place. On one hand, the mission has money, supplies, and a working means of communication with the SD offices in Berlin. On the other hand, they've just buried the chopped-up remains of their most experienced member.

For this struggling team of undercover agents, more surprises are on the way.

18

Moscow, Soviet Union

— MAY 20, 1943 —

He's about to be face-to-face with "The Man of Steel." Uniformed aides usher President Roosevelt's envoy, Joseph Davies, into a large, ornate office at the heart of the Kremlin—the fortified complex in central Moscow that houses and protects the Soviet government. There, Davies finds himself facing Molotov, the Soviet Foreign Minister; an unnamed interpreter; and Joseph Stalin, the Premier of the Soviet Union.

Davies knows that the Soviets like to get right to the point, so he makes a few rehearsed remarks, which the interpreter translates. The President and the American people, he says, are "unequivocally devoted to winning the war over Hitler and the [Japanese] and preserving the peace of the world from the threat of either Hitler or the Axis."

The Soviet Premier is known to be a man of few words who's difficult to read in person. He rarely engages in small talk or reveals what he is thinking. As Davies talks, Stalin doodles on a piece of blank paper, apparently listening but not looking at Davies or the others in the room.

Former US Ambassador to the Soviet Union Joseph Davies (*left*) meets with Soviet Premier Joseph Stalin (*right*) in the Kremlin during Davies's visit to Moscow in May 1943. (Sovfoto/Universal Images Group/Shutterstock)

Roosevelt's primary reason for sending him, Davies goes on, is to urge a personal meeting between the two leaders. He hands Roosevelt's letter to the interpreter so they can read it to Molotov and Stalin. As the interpreter reads and translates, Stalin maintains what Davies calls a "grim face," and all the while he keeps doodling.

Only once does Stalin stop and interrupt. It's the part where Roosevelt makes clear that Churchill isn't invited. "Why?" asks Stalin, clearly surprised.

Following Roosevelt's instructions, Davies explains that the American and Soviet leaders will likely be able to reach an agreement faster and understand each other better in a one-on-one setting. Roosevelt will then fill Churchill in on every part of the discussion.

Stalin doesn't respond.

The interpreter continues reading the letter and soon reaches the end, concluding with Roosevelt's colloquial send-off, "You are doing a grand job. Good luck!"

Stalin, still doodling, asks Davies a few foreign-policy questions, which Davies does his best to answer. Then Stalin is silent again. He seems to be thinking. Finally, he puts his pen down and looks up at Davies.

"I think your President is right," he says. "You may tell your President I agree with him, and it is necessary that we meet, as he suggests." Stalin then asks for an aide to bring him a map and a ruler.

With the map in front of him, he begins measuring distances on it. After completing a few measurements, he says he agrees with Roosevelt's suggestion that Alaska is a fair midpoint between the two nations' capitals and goes on to promise that within a day or two he'll have a letter of his own for Davies to carry back to Washington, DC.

For now, they all agree to maintain silence about what has been said in their meeting.

Davies leaves knowing he's done exactly as Roosevelt asked. The next day, he sends a cable to the President indicating that he met with Stalin and Molotov and that the President's letter "seemed to be favorably and cordially received."

A few days later, as promised, Stalin and Molotov present Davies with a letter that he is to hand-deliver to Roosevelt. They also add some personal gifts from the Soviet Premier to the President. Where other world leaders might give works of art or national culinary delicacies, Stalin sends a Soviet tommy gun and a captured German light hand machine gun.

Davies's trip home takes a full ten days since he can only fly through friendly airspace. Finally, on June 3, roughly a month after he departed, he arrives back in Washington and hands the letter from Stalin to Roosevelt.

In his letter, Stalin gets right to the point as usual. "I agree with you that such a meeting is necessary and that it should not be postponed," the letter states. "Therefore I would suggest that our meeting should be arranged in July or in August."

Roosevelt is pleased to read this, because this timing works for him, too.

"If you agree to this," the letter continues, "I undertake to inform you two weeks before the date of the meeting when this meeting could take place."

In other words, based on developments on the Eastern Front, Stalin will give Roosevelt two weeks' notice to arrange the trip.

"As to the place of the meeting," Stalin writes, "this will be communicated to you by Mr. Davies personally." It's clear that Stalin believes the location should be so secret that he can't even put it in a hand-delivered letter.

After reading this line, Roosevelt looks up. Davies explains that Stalin measured the distances on a map and agreed to Alaska as a potential meeting place.

Roosevelt's unusual strategy of sending an envoy to Moscow seems to have paid off. Stalin will meet with him in person, within a reasonable time frame, at the location that Roosevelt had suggested.

"Joe, you have done a grand job," Roosevelt says to Davies.

On the surface, it sounds like the mission was a success.

But there is a problem.

Roosevelt will have to inform Churchill that he has made plans to meet with Stalin without him, and that he kept this planning a secret even while the two of them were spending the past few weeks together. And Churchill will work out that at the very moment he was telling Congress that he and Roosevelt were seeking a Big Three meeting with Stalin, Roosevelt was making different plans with Stalin behind Churchill's back. It will signal to Churchill that Roosevelt doesn't entirely trust him—or, worse, that the United States is attempting to make a plan with Stalin that is not in Britain's best interest.

It's a bad time for a potential rift. Although the President and the Prime Minister got along well during Churchill's visit, the talks between the American and British war planners were sometimes heated, even acrimonious.

As usual, the issue was where to focus the US and British military effort in Europe. Churchill was determined to double down on the Mediterranean "soft underbelly" strategy and was negative about the prospects of a direct attack against Nazi Germany across the English Channel into northern France. The Allies had just spent the past year clearing North Africa of Axis troops. Having done so, it would be foolish not to seize the opportunity to cross the Mediterranean and invade Italy via Sicily. This would give them a chance to knock Italy out of the war.

But there's no way they can do that and attack northern France across the Channel at the same time. That's why the United States agrees with the British plan: to prioritize the "Southern Strategy" at the expense of opening a second front in Western Europe. The cross-Channel attack will have to wait until the next calendar year.

On June 2, the day before Davies arrives back in Washington with Stalin's letter, Roosevelt and Churchill send a message to the Soviet Premier with a summary of their plans. They set out what they will be doing for the remainder of 1943: "In the Mediterranean, the decision was made to eliminate Italy from the war as quickly as possible," the message states, explaining their plan to invade Italy in the summer. This will require most of the British and American forces in the region, and, as a result, "the concentration of forces and landing equipment in the

British Isles should proceed at a rate to permit a full-scale invasion of the Continent to be launched . . . in the spring of 1944."

For Stalin, it's the year that will jump out. The cross-Channel attack won't be happening until 1944. By this point, he has already waited impatiently for a year and a half for the Americans and British to strike at Hitler's armies in Western Europe and thereby give the Soviets relief from the Nazi onslaught. Now, Roosevelt and Churchill are saying that the Soviet Union will have to weather the storm for another full year.

So, while Roosevelt is reading the letter that Davies brought him from Moscow, he's also aware that Stalin is about to read a message he won't like at all.

Roosevelt and Churchill thought Stalin would be *disappointed* that the cross-Channel attack into northern France would be delayed for another year. But Stalin isn't disappointed. He's *furious.* After receiving Roosevelt and Churchill's message, Stalin writes them back, on June 11, with a long and detailed response. As expected, he zeroes in on one thing: the delay in the timing of the cross-Channel attack.

He starts by laying out the many times in the past they have promised the attack and failed to deliver. As for this latest delay,

> Your decision creates exceptional difficulties for the Soviet Union, which, straining all its resources, for the past two years, has been engaged against the main forces of Germany and her satellites, and leaves the Soviet Army, which is fighting not only for its country, but also for its Allies, to do the job alone, almost single-handed, against an enemy that is still very strong and formidable.

The term "single-handed" is a bit rich, given that the United States has been supplying the Soviets with planes, tanks, weapons, and raw materials while also fighting a war against Japan on the other side of the globe. Not to mention the fact that the Americans and the British have been engaged against the Axis powers in North Africa for a year and are now about to attack Italy via Sicily.

Churchill bristles at Stalin's message. In a long response that Roosevelt agrees to cosign, he lists the risks and difficulties of the cross-Channel attack and argues that it would be foolish to attempt it before the end of the year:

> I quite understand your disappointment but I am sure we are doing not only the right thing but the only thing that is physically possible in the circumstances. It would be no help to Russia if we threw away a hundred thousand men in a disastrous cross-Channel attack such as would, in my opinion, certainly occur if we tried under present conditions . . . I cannot see how a great British defeat and slaughter would aid the Soviet armies.

Churchill's fear of losing one hundred thousand men may ring hollow to the Soviet leader, whose country, by that point, had sacrificed ten million lives to the war.

Not surprisingly, Churchill's message is not well received. Stalin writes another long response, even more strongly worded than the first. Again, he recounts the many times the British and the Americans have reneged on their promise. Then he goes further: "You say that you 'quite understand' my disappointment. I must tell you that the point here is not just the disappointment of the Soviet government, but the preservation of its confidence in its Allies, a confidence which is being subjected to severe stress."

These are loaded words, and Stalin knows it.

Since the start of the partnership, one of Roosevelt and Churchill's great fears is that if Stalin was able to obtain a decisive military advantage over the Nazi armies now in the Soviet Union, he might use his leverage to negotiate a separate peace directly with Germany on terms favorable to him. For example, the Soviet Union might demand its conquered territory back but allow Germany to maintain control over Western Europe. That would leave a strong Nazi Germany controlling Western Europe and a weak and isolated Great Britain.

It would be the opposite of what Roosevelt called for at the Casablanca conference: Namely, that the Axis powers must be defeated completely, that they must surrender unconditionally, and that their fascist regimes be destroyed forever.

This is a precarious moment. By saying that the Soviet government's "confidence in its Allies" is being "subjected to severe stress," Stalin is making it clear that he's prepared to leave the alliance if the United States and the UK fail to keep their promises. And, as he has stated in two consecutive messages, this is precisely what he believes they have done.

Responding with another angry message, Churchill reminds Stalin that at the start of the war, "we British were left alone to face the worst that Nazi Germany could do to us," and yet they still gave aid to the Soviet Union after Hitler launched his surprise invasion. "I am satisfied that I have done everything in human power to help you," Churchill's message continues. "Therefore, the reproaches which you now cast upon your Western Allies leave me unmoved."

Churchill, always short-tempered, is now in his own full rage. He tells some aides that after this last message, his communication with Stalin might be over for good. A few months ago, the Big Three alliance seemed stable and strong. Now, at this critical juncture, their unity is crumbling. The Churchill and Stalin relationship, troubled from the start, is in flames.

If ever there was a time for Roosevelt to step up and pull the Allies back together, this is it. The tricky thing is that it won't be easy. At this point, Roosevelt doesn't have credibility with Stalin, who's still angry about the cross-Channel delay. With Churchill, he has a reservoir of trust, but that may evaporate when Roosevelt reveals he's been trying to make plans with Stalin behind Churchill's back.

In fact, when it comes to telling Churchill about his clandestine plan with Stalin, Roosevelt can't bring himself to do it, either face-to-face or in writing. Instead, he sends a diplomat, Averell Harriman, to London to break the news of the President's plan.

As expected, Churchill isn't happy. "I must emphasize his disappointment," Harriman reports to Roosevelt the next day. In addition to feeling betrayed, Churchill thinks that the British people will view a one-on-one meeting between Roosevelt and Stalin as publicly humiliating to Churchill, or, worse yet, as an insult to Britain's war effort.

No question, the triumvirate is falling apart. Stalin is furious at Roosevelt and Churchill for breaking their promise on the cross-Channel attack. Roosevelt has offended Churchill by planning to meet with Stalin behind his back. And the United States and the UK are genuinely concerned that the Soviet Union might abandon its partners.

The day after his meeting with Harriman, Churchill is clearly still stewing as he writes a carefully worded message to Roosevelt. "Averell told me last night of your wish for a meeting with U. J. in Alaska *à deux*," the message begins.

Who's "U. J."? It's shorthand for "Uncle Joe," a

nickname that Churchill and Roosevelt sometimes use for Stalin when writing to each other.

Having opened with a reminder of the informality between them, Churchill proceeds to lay out the case for why he disagrees with Roosevelt's plan for a one-on-one meeting.

> The whole world is expecting and all our side are desiring a meeting of the three great powers . . . It would seem a pity to draw U. J. 7,000 miles from Moscow for anything less than this . . . I consider that a tripartite meeting . . . not only of us three but also of the staffs, who will come together for the first time, would be one of the milestones of history. If this is lost, much is lost.

Churchill goes on to explain: "I do not underrate the use that enemy propaganda would make of a meeting between the heads of Soviet Russia and the United States at this juncture with the British Commonwealth and Empire excluded. It would be serious and vexatious, and many would be bewildered and alarmed thereby."

Three days later, Roosevelt responds. His message begins with a striking sentence: "I did not suggest to UJ that we meet alone but he told Davies that he assumed . . . that we would meet alone."

This is striking because it is simply not true. Roosevelt was the one who suggested to Stalin that they have a one-on-one, and, as Davies witnessed, Stalin was surprised and taken aback that Churchill would not be invited.

"Of course, you and I are completely frank in matters of this kind," the President's message continues, compounding his dishonesty by specifically alluding to the history of trust between them.

Clearly, Roosevelt's fabrication is an attempt to save face with Churchill, perhaps assuming there's no way the Prime Minister will ever learn the truth. Still, it prompts the question, why would Roosevelt lie, potentially undermining the loyalty between them?

The likely answer is simple pragmatism. For Roosevelt, winning the war is the absolute priority. He genuinely believes that a one-on-one meeting between himself and Stalin is in the best interests of the war effort, so he does what he can to set it up. He also knows that maintaining Churchill's goodwill is critical to the alliance, so he says what he can to appease the Prime Minister. When a war is raging and millions of innocent people are being slaughtered, a question of personal honesty between two individuals may not be so important.

Roosevelt's fabrication works. Churchill is appeased—at least for the moment. However, the two leaders still have a problem. Stalin is so furious that it looks like the chances of a face-to-face meeting—whether one-on-one or all three together—have all but disappeared.

19

Berlin, Germany

— LATE JULY 1943 —

For the intelligence chief, spy craft is a passion.

Walter Schellenberg delights in the technical details of intelligence work: wiretaps, surveillance, ciphers, and signals interception. Every few weeks, he hosts a dinner party at his home for the technical heads of the various German intelligence departments, where they all share techniques and ideas. “These meetings,” Schellenberg later reported, “were perhaps more than any other single factor responsible for the high standard of the scientific and technical side of my service.”

Within the labyrinth of the German intelligence

organizations, one of the most secretive agencies—and the one that Schellenberg and other leaders rely on the most—is the Forschungsamt, roughly translated as the "Research Agency," and often abbreviated as the FA.

Unlike the other intelligence services, which are frequently driven by political, military, and ideological agendas, the FA is a highly technical organization that focuses entirely on tapping telecommunications lines, intercepting enemy signals and radio transmissions, and breaking ciphers and codes. It doesn't interpret the information it receives; it just gathers it, decrypts the codes, translates the material, and organizes the results to be distributed, daily, in what are known as "Brown Sheets" because of the light-brown paper they are printed on.

Only a select few in the upper echelons of Nazi leadership are allowed to receive Brown Sheets. They are so sensitive, in fact, that they are transported in locked pouches. Each sheet is carefully accounted for by the FA, and the recipient must return them within one month to be permanently destroyed.

On the rare occasion in which the contents of these sheets are revealed beyond their audience of upper-level Nazi leaders, it is usually because one of the recipients has written about them. For example, one regular recipient of the FA's Brown Sheets is Joseph Goebbels, the Reich Minister of Propaganda and one of Hitler's closest confidants. Because Goebbels kept regular voluminous diaries, some details of the FA's work are contained in his diary entries and known to us today. These entries reveal, among other things, that the agency was sometimes able to intercept Allied communications at the highest levels—including those involving Roosevelt, Churchill, and Stalin. Since the Casablanca conference in early 1943, the FA has been intercepting clues related to the planning of an Allied conference later in the year, this time to include Roosevelt and Stalin.

How exactly the FA obtained the top secret decrypts regarding Roosevelt's intention to meet Stalin one-on-one is unknown, but Schellenberg would later brag about the systems by which the Nazis monitored US and British communications:

> We succeeded in tapping the main cable between England and America. The word "tapping" is used here in a figurative sense. In spite of the insulation of the cable we were able, by the use of shortwave instruments, to record the high-frequency impulses running

through it, and by an incredibly complicated process to decipher them.

One night in late July 1943, Schellenberg has a meeting with Admiral Wilhelm Canaris, the head of the Abwehr, Germany's military intelligence agency. Unlike Schellenberg's SD, which was created by the SS and answers directly to Hitler, the Abwehr predates the Nazi Party and maintains at least some independence. For this reason, the two agencies are sometimes considered rivals.

Canaris is an intelligence veteran, much older than Schellenberg, and he and Schellenberg maintain an open communication. Recently, the two men have been collaborating with some frequency, specifically on the operations involving Iran.

Operation Anton, the latest mission into Iranian tribal regions outside Tehran, requires German paratroopers to connect with an Abwehr agent on the ground—just like Operation Franz involved paratroopers linking up with SD agent Franz Mayr. While Operation Anton is technically an Abwehr mission, it is being overseen by the new special operations leader Otto Skorzeny, whom Schellenberg recently hired on behalf of the SD. For that reason, it's essentially a shared operation between the two agencies.

Tonight, as the spymasters sip their drinks, they have much to talk about—not just about Iran but also about Germany's increasingly troubled prospects in the war. Canaris also has a specific message to impart to Schellenberg. Hitler, he tells him, has taken particular interest in rumors about a Big Three conference supposedly in the planning stages.

By this point in July 1943, it doesn't take secret intelligence to know that such a meeting is being discussed. There has been open speculation about a Big Three summit in the Allied press since the spring, and it has been something of an international guessing game to predict if, when, and where such an event might take place.

Six months ago, the German intelligence services got it wrong when it came to Casablanca. Not just wrong, but very wrong. According to Canaris, Hitler does not want this to happen again. If there's to be a Big Three summit, the Führer wants to know in advance when and where it will take place.

Since the few crumbs of information about a proposed meeting were intercepted back in spring, the German agencies have learned no further details. If there is to be a Big Three summit in 1943, they haven't the slightest idea about the timing or location.

These two men, Schellenberg and Canaris, have enormous resources at their disposal. They have the apparatus and staffs of their respective intelligence agencies. They have access to the daily reports from the FA. And they have a directive that comes from Hitler himself.

For these Nazi intelligence leaders, the mission is clear: Find out where the Big Three will meet—and this time, don't get it wrong.

20

Washington, DC

— JULY 1943 —

Roosevelt needs Stalin back.

Although FDR technically cosigned Churchill's messages during the British Prime Minister's angry exchanges with Stalin, he was careful not to enter the fray himself. Roosevelt always believed, and still believes, that maintaining goodwill with the Soviet Union—in other words, goodwill with Stalin—is essential to the war effort.

For that reason, on June 16, while Churchill and Stalin were sending angry letters to each other, Roosevelt quietly sent a separate message to Stalin regarding US airpower shipments:

> In addition to our new protocol agreement, I have directed that six hundred additional fighters be sent to you during the balance of 1943. They are P-40N type of fighter... This is the most maneuverable fighter we have. It provides our best protection against dive bombers and gives excellent protection to the ground strafing of the P-39s. I have also directed the shipment of seventy-eight additional B-25s during the same period.

Now he's speaking Stalin's language. Several days later, on June 22, Roosevelt wrote another message to Stalin, marking the two-year anniversary of Hitler's invasion of the Soviet Union and commending the Soviet defense:

> Two years ago tomorrow, by an act of treachery in keeping with the long record of Nazi duplicity the Nazi leaders launched their brutal attack upon the Soviet Union...During the

> past two years the freedom-loving peoples of the world have watched with increasing admiration the history making exploits of the armed forces of the Soviet Union and the almost incredible sacrifices which the Russian people are so heroically making.

Roosevelt's words, and the promise of American fighter planes, were designed to soften the Soviet Premier's anger. Through a mix of flattery and regular arms shipments, he's hoping to bring Stalin back from the brink.

Ultimately, though, it's a series of global military events that mend the bad feelings and disagreements within the alliance—more than any letter from Roosevelt ever could. In early July 1943, Germany launches Operation Citadel, a huge tank-based offensive designed to overwhelm Soviet armies near the city of Kursk in Russia. Unbeknownst to the Germans, a combination of Soviet and British intelligence has given the Allies advance knowledge of the German attack plan. The Red Army has prepared a meticulous defense, including a surprise counteroffensive to be launched after the first wave of German attacks.

The attack begins on July 5, and what transpires over the next several days becomes known as the largest tank battle in world history. The entire region is overwhelmed by tanks swarming the countryside from all directions, swallowing nearby towns and villages. "It wasn't a battle, it was a slaughterhouse of tanks . . . Everything was enveloped in smoke, dust and fire," one Red Army commander remembered. Losses are tremendous on both sides: over two hundred thousand Germans and eight hundred thousand Soviets. Despite the immense Soviet losses, after two weeks of fighting the Red Army has held its ground and prevented the Wehrmacht from advancing. For the Germans, Operation Citadel is largely a failure.

Seizing on the good news, Roosevelt uses it as another opportunity to make amends with Stalin. "Although I have no detailed news, I think I can safely congratulate you on the splendid showing your armies are making against the German offensive at Kursk," he writes in a short note on July 15. He adds, almost as an aside, "I hope to hear from you very soon about the other matter which I still feel to be of great importance to you and me."

He is referring, of course, to their meeting. It's been nearly six weeks since there has been any mention of the one-on-one summit. Stalin's fury about the delayed cross-Channel attack shut down the discussion. Now Roosevelt sees a chance to revive it.

What's also helpful is that, at nearly exactly the same time as the massive battle around Kursk is going on, the British, American, and Canadian forces in North Africa are crossing the Mediterranean and launching their planned invasion of the Italian island of Sicily.

Code-named Operation Husky, it represents the first major American and British attack against Axis ground forces on European soil since the United States entered the war. The first Allied troops land in Sicily on July 10, where they meet stiff resistance from Italian and German troops. But the Allies' careful planning and superior naval and air power prevail, and soon American and British forces hold key cities and ports. Within days, the remaining Axis troops are forced to evacuate.

Even Stalin, who has always held the Mediterranean campaign in contempt, can see that the victory in Sicily represents a shift in momentum. Churchill and Roosevelt are sure to tell him that the attack on Sicily is forcing Hitler to divert troops from the Eastern Front that might otherwise have fought against the Red Army during Operation Citadel.

Even more remarkable is the impact that the capture of

Sicily is having on Italian morale. For the past year, Italy's army has been performing poorly. The Italian people have lost faith in their fascist government and in the Axis alliance. Many are wondering why their country is engaged in a dangerous war to support Germany's territorial ambitions. The Italian government falls into chaos, torn between sticking with the German alliance and trying to make a deal with the Allies. The pro-Allies faction takes the lead, but they quickly realize they will not get a chance to negotiate with the British and Americans so long as Mussolini, Hitler's fascist ally, remains in power.

In a series of extraordinary events, the Italian monarch, King Victor Emmanuel III, summons Mussolini to the palace and informs him that he is to be stripped of power. When the stunned dictator exits the building, he is surrounded by armed *carabinieri*—royal guards—and taken into custody. Benito Mussolini, who has ruled Italy for nearly twenty years and who once seemed invincible, is now taken away in the back of a van like a common criminal.

As the world learns of these dramatic events, fighting is continuing along the Eastern Front. On August 4, Soviet troops achieve an enormous psychological victory when they recapture Orel, a city the Germans invaded in October

1941 and which they have occupied ever since. Orel has been mostly destroyed—its original population of 114,000 is now only 30,000—but at least it is back in Soviet hands.

Determined to capitalize on the good news, Roosevelt continues his charm offensive on Stalin. "Sincere congratulations to the Red Army, the People of the Soviet Union and to yourself upon the great victory of Orel . . . The Soviet Union can be justly proud of its heroic accomplishments." He doesn't mention the issue of the face-to-face summit, which Stalin still hasn't responded to.

But four days later, on August 8, Stalin replies: "Thank you for your congratulation sent on the Red Army and the Soviet people on the occasion of successes at Orel." Then he brings up his promise and explains why it has been difficult for him to follow through:

> I have at the present time to put aside other questions and my other duties, except the primary duty—the direction of action at the front . . . I hope that under such circumstances you will fully understand that at the present time I cannot go on a long journey and shall not be able,

> unfortunately, during this summer and autumn to keep my promise given to you through Mr. Davies.
>
> I regret it very much, but, as you know, circumstances are sometimes more powerful than people who are compelled to submit to them.

This is not what Roosevelt was hoping to hear, but, as he reads on, he sees that Stalin is only rejecting the time and place, not the idea of the meeting itself. In fact, Stalin explains, "I consider that a meeting of the responsible representatives of our countries would positively be expedient." A comment later in the same letter is even more interesting:

> I do not have any objections to the presence of Mr. Churchill at this meeting, in order that the meeting of the representatives of the two countries would become the meeting of the representatives of the three countries. I still follow this point

of view on the condition that you
will not have any objections to this.

In other words, despite Stalin's personal distrust of Churchill, he has apparently decided that if any of them should meet, they should *all* meet: a team of three. Perhaps he is making an effort to put aside his differences with Churchill. Or perhaps it's more practical: He only wants to make one trip, so better to have all three of them present.

Almost all the specifics that Roosevelt proposed via Joseph Davies have been overturned. The date of a potential meeting is now later, the location has changed, and the possibility of a one-on-one meeting has seemingly evaporated. Still, Roosevelt knows good news when he sees it. At the end of the day, the most important thing is this: The plan for a face-to-face meeting between the Allied leaders seems to be back in play.

Assuming nothing gets in the way.

21

Berlin, Germany

— JULY 26, 1943 —

Otto Skorzeny, Captain of the Waffen-SS, is bored.

As a soldier used to fighting in the field, he's frustrated by the office politics and infighting of the SD and other agencies within the Reich Security Main Office. "I must say," he later wrote, "that if I had suspected in advance all the intrigues, the narrow-mindedness and the clumsiness of the bureaucracy, I would probably never have accepted this commando post."

He's feeling particularly listless on the afternoon of July 26. He's in a restaurant in Berlin, having just finished a long lunch with a former classmate, catching up and talking about old friends. He's wearing civilian clothes, not anticipating anything of importance to happen that day. Because several hours have passed since he left his office, he calls to check in and is surprised when his secretary answers the phone in a "state of wild excitement."

She explains hurriedly that everyone on his staff has been looking for him for the past two hours. Why the commotion? "FHQ has sent for you, chief. A plane will be waiting for you at five o'clock at the Tempelhofer airfield," she answers.

Skorzeny takes a moment to make sure he's heard correctly. FHQ stands for "Führer Headquarters."

That's *Hitler's* headquarters in the Wolf's Lair.

For anyone serving the Reich, it's an honor to be summoned there—and usually the sign of something important.

Trying to conceal his excitement, Skorzeny calmly asks the secretary, "Is there any hint as to what it's all about?"

"No," she replies, "we know nothing at all."

Skorzeny tells the secretary to have his uniform sent to the airfield and heads there directly himself. As his driver races him across the city, he tries to figure out why he's been summoned. "Could it be connected with 'Operation Franz'?" he wonders, but decides it is not likely. He can't think of anything else he's involved in that could rise to the level of being flown to Hitler's headquarters in East Prussia.

At the airport, he meets the aide who has brought his uniform. They hear some chatter among the airport staff about the surprise downfall of Mussolini—this dramatic news has just broken—but don't pay it much mind. On the tarmac, a massive Junkers Ju 52 aircraft is waiting, and, once inside, Skorzeny sees that he's the only passenger. This huge plane is just for him.

After a three-hour flight, the Junkers lands on a small airstrip deep in the Prussian woods, where a large Mercedes sedan is waiting.

"Are you Captain Skorzeny?" a sergeant asks. "I'm here to take you to headquarters at once." With Skorzeny in the back seat, the driver races for several miles along winding roads through forests and fields. It's getting dark when they arrive at a compound of buildings. Inside, Skorzeny discovers that he is one of six military officers who have been summoned to the Wolf's Lair. Now they all wait together.

The others are Colonels and Majors, and all of them outrank Skorzeny, a Captain. Two are from the Wehrmacht, two from the Luftwaffe, and the other is a fellow Waffen-SS officer. No one appears to know why they're there.

A uniformed aide appears and announces, "I'll take you to the Führer, gentlemen."

"I . . . trembled in every limb," Skorzeny later recalled.

He is right to be excited. He's about to be face-to-face with Adolf Hitler.

22

The Wolf's Lair, East Prussia

— JULY 26, 1943 —

The six uniformed officers stand at attention. They form a straight line, side by side, in a dimly lit room with dark curtains and maps on the walls. They all stare directly ahead.

Captain Otto Skorzeny, the lowest in rank, is the farthest to the left.

They've been standing here for a few minutes, waiting. Can it possibly be true? Are they really about to meet the Führer?

Skorzeny hears a door open. He and the others click

their heels and stand at attention. After so much anticipation, the tension is almost unbearable.

"Now I was to meet the man," Skorzeny remembered, "who had played so great a part in German history."

Adolf Hitler enters the room and immediately starts asking questions of the highest-ranking officer, who's on the far end of the line. Then he moves along the line, one by one, asking each officer several quick questions about their military backgrounds. Finally, he stands in front of Skorzeny. He asks him some basic questions about his past and his rank. Skorzeny tries to answer but struggles to maintain composure. "His word, his bearing, the entire man radiated an extraordinary power."

Then, Hitler addresses all the officers at once, surprising them with a question: "What do you think of Italy?" The other officers mumble generic statements about Italy's role as an Axis partner. Then . . .

"I am Austrian, my Führer!" Skorzeny exclaims loudly, interrupting everyone else.

The room goes silent, Skorzeny's words hanging in the air.

Why does Skorzeny make this loud statement?

As everyone in the Reich knows, Hitler is also from

Austria. And Austria has its own distinct history. At the end of World War I, a beloved part of the country was granted to Italy, and, while Italy may now be a close ally, the matter remains a grievance to native Austrians. Always a fast thinker, Skorzeny sees an opportunity to bond with Hitler over their shared background.

The question is, will the strategy work?

Immediately, Hitler walks back down along the line and stands in front of Skorzeny, staring at him intently. Then he declares, "The other gentlemen may go. I want you to stay, Captain Skorzeny."

Now Skorzeny is alone, facing the German leader. Hitler no longer seems interested in interrogating him. Instead, he begins to explain what this highly unusual meeting is about.

"Mussolini was betrayed yesterday," Hitler says. "His king had him arrested. But the Duce is not only my great ally, he is also my friend . . . and I cannot abandon this statesman."

What does this have to do with Skorzeny? Hitler explains:

We must find out where the Duce is being held and free him. That is the mission I have for you

> *Skorzeny. And I have chosen you because I am convinced that you will succeed with this operation. And you must risk everything to carry out this action, which is now most important to the conduct of the war. Naturally this mission is to be kept absolutely secret, otherwise it will fail . . . But you must act quickly, very quickly! You will understand that the life of the Duce depends on it!*

This is why Skorzeny has been summoned to the Wolf's Lair. Hitler needs a special operations expert to lead this secret mission, to discover where Mussolini is being held, and to free him.

"The longer Hitler spoke, the more I could feel his influence upon me," Skorzeny later wrote. "His words seemed to me so convincing that at that moment I had not the slightest doubt about the success of the project. There was such a warm, human inflection in his voice when he spoke of his loyalty to his Italian friend that I was deeply moved."

Hitler stares at Skorzeny for a long moment. "I have full confidence in you, Skorzeny. I hope I shall hear from you soon and wish you the best of luck."

Skorzeny can only mutter, "I fully understand, my Führer, and will do my best."

They shake hands, then Hitler's aide leads Skorzeny out of the room. His head is buzzing. The Führer himself just gave him a mission wilder than any fictional spy story. He must learn where Hitler's closest ally, Benito Mussolini, is being held—then lead the commando raid to rescue him.

For this dedicated Nazi soldier, it's the assignment of a lifetime.

23

Tehran, Iran

— AUGUST 14, 1943 —

For months, they've been hunting Nazis.

Much of the work has been tedious: sorting through paperwork and filing detailed reports. Now they're ready for action.

Tonight, just after nightfall on August 14, 1943, a group of armed British officers are on the move. With them are two Iranians. One is a member of the Persian Army Reserve, the other a lieutenant of the Persian police. What they have in common is that the British recently identified them as operatives of the underground pro-Nazi movement in Tehran—Franz Mayr's organization. Two nights ago, the British agents apprehended one of the men. After interrogation, he admitted that he was guilty of "actively participating in German activities." He led them to the second man, giving the British two self-confessed Nazi collaborators.

The British don't really care about these two locals. They want those who are higher up the chain of command. More specifically, they want notorious Nazi spy Franz Mayr, who's known to be the ringleader of the group. So, at this very moment, these two Iranians are leading the British officers to what is supposed to be a secret Nazi safehouse.

Are their informants telling the truth? Do they really have solid intelligence, or are they making empty promises in the hope of saving themselves? The British agents are about to find out.

They burst through the door of the house and within minutes find a German-made wireless transmitter and, more importantly, the young man who is there to operate it. Unlike the two informers, this man is not local. He has light-brown hair, blue eyes, and European features. As the British soon find out, he is SS Corporal Werner Rockstroh, one of the five surviving parachutists of the Operation Franz mission from Berlin.

Even better, the British learn that Rockstroh is expecting visitors later that night. For the next several hours, the officers wait, making sure that the house bears no sign of unusual activity visible from the outside. Sure enough, not one but two visitors arrive separately to meet with Rockstroh. Despite a scuffle with one of the men, they are both promptly arrested and taken in for questioning.

It's a huge score for British intelligence.

24

Quebec City, Canada

— AUGUST 21, 1943 —

The war is moving fast, and there are critical decisions to make.

Just three months after Churchill's visit to Washington, Roosevelt, Churchill, and their staffs meet again. This time, they are in Quebec City, in Canada.

After the successful invasion of Sicily and the fall of Mussolini, the most pressing issues concern military strategy along the Mediterranean front. Germany has rushed troops to the Italian mainland to defend against a possible Allied attack. The Italian King and Grand Council are prepared to abandon the Axis powers and make a deal with the UK and the United States. The Italian army is divided, with some factions planning to fight with the Germans and some ready to switch sides. It's a chaotic situation that demands complex decision-making.

Churchill has always favored the Mediterranean campaign, so at the Quebec summit he pushes hard for a plan to follow up the Sicilian campaign with an invasion of the Italian mainland that will push the Axis forces out of the country. Roosevelt supports him in this.

The Mediterranean strategy isn't the only priority. Roosevelt insists that they also plan for the cross-Channel attack into northern France. Once again, debates between the Americans and the British are heated. Churchill's constant wavering, which only a few months ago nearly pushed Stalin out of the alliance, continues to aggravate the Americans.

Every time an agreement seems close, Churchill or one of his advisers presents a new idea to delay or downgrade the cross-Channel attack in favor of the Southern Strategy. This time, however, Roosevelt holds firm. Churchill and the British must stick to what they agreed together and subsequently shared with Stalin: an invasion of northern France in the spring of 1944. After much back and forth, the Combined Chiefs of Staff outline key elements of the plan and set a target date of May 1, 1944, to launch the cross-Channel attack. Simply putting this date on paper gives military commanders a deadline to work toward and allows planning to commence.

Roosevelt and his staff push for one more important concession from the British, namely, that an American commander be the one to lead the cross-Channel attack. They don't have faith that the British leadership is truly committed to the plan and want the US military to take the lead.

The leaders need to come up with a good name for the mission, and when it comes to names, well, that's Winston Churchill's specialty. Despite all his reservations about the mission itself, the Prime Minister comes up with a winner: "Operation Overlord." Everyone likes it. From that point on, no other name is considered.

Roosevelt has another priority for the Quebec conference: namely to push aggressively for a meeting with Stalin. To this end, the two leaders write a cosigned message to the Soviet leader:

> We wish to emphasize once more the importance of a meeting between all three of us . . . The present seems to

be a unique opportunity for a rendezvous and also a crucial point in the war. We earnestly hope that you will give this matter once more your consideration.

On August 24, just as the Quebec conference is wrapping up, Stalin responds to Roosevelt and Churchill's request for a meeting. By the time his message arrives, they are both leaving Quebec, so each reads the reply separately: "I entirely share your opinion . . . about the importance of a meeting between the three of us."

Roosevelt sends a quick note to Churchill: "I hope you have seen Uncle Joe's new message which is greatly improved in its tone . . . My first feeling is that he has come around to our secondary meeting and that it should be held very soon."

Roosevelt and Churchill decide not to press the issue right away and instead send Stalin another message, filling him in on the rest of the details from their conference. This includes an update on the subject closest to Stalin's heart: the cross-Channel attack into northern France, now officially planned for the following spring.

"A large-scale buildup of American forces in the United

Kingdom is now underway," they tell him. "It will provide an initial assault force of British and American divisions for cross-Channel operations." They don't share the exact launch date with Stalin—they probably don't want to be held to it—but state emphatically that "this operation will be the primary British and American ground and air effort against the Axis."

A week after the conference, on August 31, Churchill takes to the airwaves to give a lengthy public address about the war effort. He specifically raises the subject of a proposed Big Three meeting and applies strong public pressure on Stalin to engage:

> Nothing is nearer to the wishes of President Roosevelt and myself than to have a threefold meeting with Marshal Stalin. If that has not yet taken place it is certainly not because we have not tried our best or have not been willing to lay aside impediment and undertake further immense journeys for that purpose . . . The President and I will persevere in our efforts to meet Marshal Stalin.

A few days later, on September 4, Roosevelt sends the Soviet leader a message bringing up the summit one more time. "I still hope that you and Mr. Churchill and I can meet as soon as possible. I personally could arrange to meet in a place as far as North Africa between November fifteenth and December fifteenth."

Roosevelt and Churchill have now asked Stalin a half dozen times in just a few weeks. That's in addition to their many requests during the summer *and* Roosevelt's elaborate ploy of sending a special envoy to Moscow *and* their pleading with the Soviet Premier to join them for the Casablanca conference and then for another proposed meeting in spring. It seems like the one question Stalin is determined to avoid.

At long last, Stalin writes back to Roosevelt on September 8. "As to our personal meeting with participation of Mr. Churchill I am also interested to have it arranged as soon as possible. Your proposal regarding the time of the meeting seems to me acceptable." He continues: "I consider that it would be expedient to choose as the place of the meeting the country where there are the representations of all three countries," he writes, adding, "for instance, Iran."

Iran?

This is a genuine surprise.

By this point, they have considered and rejected locations in Morocco, Egypt, Scotland, Norway, Russia, and Alaska. No one has ever suggested Iran.

For Roosevelt, it's complicated. On the one hand, Iran is farther from the United States than any location proposed by Roosevelt or Churchill. The United States has no infrastructure for high-level visits to the region and would have to plan logistics and security from scratch. On the other hand, Stalin is correct in saying that Iran is a nation where all three powers have representation. Because of the critical importance of the Trans-Iranian Railway, the country is relatively well secured by British and Soviet troops. Both the UK and the Soviet Union have embassies in the capital city of Tehran, and the United States has a legation—a diplomatic office lower in rank than an embassy, legations are no longer in use—there. Furthermore, the relatively remote desert location might allow for greater secrecy than most places in Europe or near the Mediterranean.

Iran.

It just might work.

25

Italy

— LATE SUMMER 1943 —

Immediately after his meeting with Hitler in the Wolf's Lair, Otto Skorzeny starts preparing for his mission to rescue Mussolini.

He calls his second-in-command, Karl Radl, and tells him that no one in the Berlin office will be sleeping that night. While he can't yet reveal the reason, he needs a commando unit ready to go the next morning. "Pick fifty men—only the best," he orders.

In addition to men, Skorzeny needs supplies, and since no one has the slightest idea where Mussolini is being held, they'll have to be ready for any sort of mission. Every soldier must be outfitted with machine guns, pistols, hand grenades, plastic explosives, fuses, helmets, rations, and both warm- and cold-weather uniforms.

The following morning, Skorzeny is on a scheduled flight from East Prussia to Rome. While in the air, he learns that fifty soldiers from Berlin are also on their way. As soon as he arrives in Rome, Skorzeny tries to find out where Mussolini is being held. German officers in the city introduce him to friendly assets within the Italian state police and to other city officials who may be able to help him.

The search soon becomes maddening. Every few days, the royal authorities move their prisoner to a different location. And every time Skorzeny's team receives intelligence that Mussolini is in one place, they soon learn that he's already been moved somewhere else.

Every time they have a lead, they make elaborate preparations. When they hear Il Duce might be on board a ship, they commandeer dozens of boats and map out a mission to storm his vessel and steer it to a German-controlled port. Later, they hear he is being held in a fortress on an isolated island and devise a complex amphibious landing to storm the island and rescue him. Neither of these rumors turns out to be true.

Meanwhile, British and American forces are bombing

Rome and other northern cities. The barracks where Skorzeny's team is staying gets badly damaged by a bomb, and they have to relocate. An Allied ground invasion of the country seems imminent. Amid this chaos, Skorzeny and his team receive compelling intelligence that the authorities have moved Mussolini to a remote ski resort in the Italian Alps, northeast of Rome.

Although Skorzeny isn't sure the intelligence is reliable, he knows that, with an Allied invasion likely to start any day, this might be their last chance to launch a rescue mission. He has no choice but to proceed in the hope that his sources are correct.

He arranges a reconnaissance flight to circle the mountains where the hotel is located and figure out how his team can reach this extremely remote target. At first, it looks like the only way to get to the hotel is by cable car. Then Skorzeny notices a triangle-shaped clearing beside the building. It appears to be an empty field or meadow. This discovery becomes the key to an unusual plan. Instead of relying on the cable car to get to the hotel, Skorzeny's commando team could use the triangular meadow near the hotel as a landing strip. No conventional aircraft could ever land on such a small and uneven space, but perhaps a lightweight, motorless glider could. That would put them within immediate striking distance of the hotel. Once Mussolini was rescued, a small, two-passenger plane could swoop down to pick him up and transport him to safety.

The glider plan also gives them the element of surprise. "It was certain that no one expected an attack from the air," was Skorzeny's reckoning. This could be their one and only chance to attempt a rescue.

After a few frantic days of preparation, they are ready. Skorzeny has secured a dozen lightweight DFS 230 gliders from the Luftwaffe, each of which can carry nine passengers and a pilot. Because an Allied bombing raid on the airfield had left craters on the runway, two of the gliders ran aground during takeoff, but the remaining ten made it into the air, with Skorzeny himself in the lead glider.

Now, roughly an hour after taking off, the gliders are approaching their destination. Through the small window, Skorzeny spots the snowy mountaintop coming into view. "Helmets on!" he yells to everyone on board.

Minutes later, the hotel itself is visible.

Yet as the aircraft approaches, something doesn't look right.

"The pilot turned in a wide circle, searching the ground . . . for the flat meadow appointed as our landing-ground," Skorzeny recalled. "But a further, and ghastly, surprise was in store for us. It was triangular all right, but so far from being flat it was a steep, a very steep hillside!"

Unable to land, the ten gliders are about to crash into the side of the mountain.

Skorzeny has only a few seconds to think. He *should* order the pilot to swerve away from the mountaintop, glide down to the valley below, and hope to land safely. In other words, he should abandon the mission. Or . . . he could do something else.

"Crash landing!" Skorzeny bellows at the top of his lungs. "As near as the hotel as you can get!" He's in charge of the aircraft—this is a direct order.

The pilot tilts the starboard wing toward the mountaintop. As the wind shrieks around them, the glider hurtles straight toward the rocky face of the rugged mountain peak.

26

Washington, DC

— SEPTEMBER 1943 —

There's new hope for the summit.

The Casablanca conference proved to Roosevelt that when national leaders meet face-to-face, it could be enormously symbolic. The photograph of him and Churchill sitting together was a powerful image of alliance and strength that was seen around the world.

And if their two-way conference in Morocco encouraged this perception of strength, then a three-way meeting with Stalin would go even further. The world had long known that Roosevelt and Churchill were closely aligned, but Stalin was another matter. So a summit of the Big Three would put the issue to rest. Not only that, it would demoralize the enemy at a key moment in the war.

The stage is now set for this to happen.

There's just one detail that keeps gnawing at Roosevelt. The location. Iran is simply too far away, and it'll take too long for him to get there. He knows he must be careful about broaching the subject with Stalin, especially considering how hard it's been to bring the Soviet leader on board for a meeting in the first place.

The day after receiving Stalin's message, he writes back. "I am delighted with your willingness to go along [with the summit]," he replies, adding, "and the time about the end of November is all right." Here's the trickier part. "My only hesitation is the place," he continues, "because it is a little bit farther from Washington than I had counted on." As an alternative, he writes, "I hope that you will consider some part of Egypt, which is also a neutral state and where every arrangement can be made for our convenience."

Unfortunately for Roosevelt, Churchill also writes to Stalin, on the same day, accepting Tehran as the location for the meeting. Brimming with excitement that the summit is happening—and that he is included—Churchill gushes, "I am pleased and relieved to feel that there is a good prospect of this taking place . . . I have for some time informed you that I will come anywhere at any time for such a meeting." The message continues, "I am therefore prepared to come to Tehran unless you can think of a better place in Iran . . . I defer to your wishes."

In response to these two simultaneous and contradictory messages, Stalin simply latches on to the one that suits him. In a message to both leaders, he writes, "As regards the meeting of the three heads of the governments, I have no objection to Tehran, which, I think, is a more suitable place than Egypt where the Soviet Union is not yet represented."

Churchill takes this as a green light. Still apparently bursting with enthusiasm, he sends Stalin another note, further affirming the choice of location. He also raises a subject of enormous importance for all three of them: security, suggesting that he make elaborate preparations to visit the city of Cairo, in Egypt, to throw off the world press. While the spotlight is on Cairo, they can secretly prepare the real location:

> Then perhaps only two or three days before our meeting we should throw a British and a Russian brigade round a suitable area in Tehran, including

the air field, and keep an absolute cordon till we have finished our talks. . . . Thus we shall have an effective blind for the world press and also for any unpleasant people who might not be as fond of us as they ought.

Churchill seems to revel in all this. Yet there's one final detail that captures the Prime Minister's attention: The conference needs a good name. Naturally, he's already given it some thought.

"The code name for the operation should be 'Eureka,'" Churchill suggests to Stalin, "which I believe is ancient Greek." He adds, "If you have other ideas let me know and we can put them to the President."

A week later, Stalin writes back regarding Churchill's idea of sending British and Russian military brigades to surround Tehran during the proposed conference. "I do not think the measure advisable—it could lead to undue commotion and exposure," Stalin argues. Instead, each country should simply "take a strong police force with them" to the summit.

Otherwise, he says, "I have no objection to the other

proposals for the coming meeting, and I agree to the code names suggested for the correspondence on the meeting."

The best strategy for security will be an ongoing question for the three leaders, but for now at least, Stalin agrees with the Prime Minister's word choice.

Eureka. The new code word for the proposed first-ever in-person meeting of the three Allied leaders during World War II.

They have a name. Now they just need to make this conference happen.

27

Gran Sasso, Italy

— SEPTEMBER 12, 1943 —

The mountain face is coming at them fast.

The glider pilot desperately scans the uneven, sloping field of rocks, looking for something—anything—that will provide a flat enough surface for a crash landing.

"I closed my eyes and stopped thinking," Skorzeny later described, as he and his team of eight SS commandos prepared for the coming crash.

During several seconds of pure commotion, there is a "frightful din" and "the noise of shattering wood" as the bottom of the glider smashes into the ground, then "bounce[s] several times" along the uneven rock face. After a "last mighty heave," the battered aircraft comes to a stop.

Thankfully realizing he's still intact, Skorzeny tumbles out of the broken hull of the aircraft onto the jagged rocks. Miraculously, the destroyed glider is now within fifteen yards of the mountaintop hotel. Barely looking back to see how the pilot or the rest of the team are doing, he grasps his machine gun in both hands and begins running toward the hotel.

Skorzeny and his men have no idea if Mussolini is even inside the building, but to maintain the advantage of surprise, they push forward with maximum speed. Behind him, he can hear the panting of some of his commandos. They're under strict orders not to fire any shots until their leader fires first and to "stick to him like glue."

A single stunned guard standing near a door is staring at them, eyes wide.

"Mani in alto!"—"Put your hands up!"—one of the Nazi commandos shouts. The guard immediately drops his weapon. The commandos smash through the door, where another guard is trying to operate a wireless radio transmitter set up on a chair. He probably ran to the radio as soon as he saw a glider hurtling toward the mountain.

Before he can send his message, Skorzeny lunges in his

direction. "A hasty kick sent his chair flying from under him," Skorzeny later described, "and a few hearty blows from my machine-pistol wrecked his apparatus."

The room has no other doors, so Skorzeny and his men race back outside and around the building, searching for entry. Skorzeny jumps up on a stone terrace, and this provides him with a perfect view of the front of the building. "My eyes swept the facade and lit on a well-known face at one of the windows of the first story. It was the Duce! Now I knew that our effort had not been in vain!"

"Duce, get away from the window!" Skorzeny shouts. Mussolini instantly recedes into the room. By remembering the location of the window, Skorzeny should now be able to go directly to Mussolini's room once he gets inside. He continues around the building until he finds the front entrance. Making sure some of his men are behind him, he storms straight in.

A handful of guards are in the foyer, but before they know what's happening, Skorzeny rushes straight through them and bounds up the staircase, three steps at a time. Relying on his judgment of the location of Mussolini's room, he charges through the second door in a long hallway.

Sure enough, there's Il Duce.

Next to him are two stunned guards. Knowing they don't stand a chance against the team of armed Nazi commandos, they drop their weapons.

"Duce, the Führer has sent me! You are free!" he exclaims.

Everything has happened so fast that the guards are simply too surprised to put up any resistance. Just four minutes after they landed, Skorzeny and his men have found and secured their target, without a single shot being fired. By now, more of the gliders have crash-landed around the mountaintop. One careened straight into a rock face and was smashed to bits, badly injuring several on board, but most of the crews have survived, and they have surrounded the hotel.

Skorzeny and a few of the other German soldiers walk Mussolini out of the room, into the hall, and down the hotel stairs. When they emerge from the front entrance, the assembled German commandos stand at attention, raising their arms in salute. A light snow has started falling, and someone takes out a camera and captures the moment.

A team of soldiers has been clearing boulders and brush to create a functional airstrip near the hotel. When it's completed, one of them waves a green light, the signal for

Skorzeny (*with binoculars*) celebrates alongside former Prime Minister Benito Mussolini (*in black*) just after Skorzeny's commando raid freed Mussolini from a remote mountaintop hotel where pro-Allied Italian forces had been holding him prisoner. (Bundesarchiv, Bild 101I-567-1503C-15/Photograph: Toni Schneiders)

a small two-engine Fieseler Storch plane that has been circling overhead to descend and land on the strip. Skorzeny and Mussolini board the tiny aircraft and brace themselves for a bumpy takeoff.

The plane accelerates along the makeshift runway and shoots off the edge of the steep mountain peak. At first, it looks like it is carrying too much weight for the thin alpine air, and its nose dips down toward the valley, but the pilot slowly rights the plane and heads away.

In a few hours, the plane will land safely in an airfield

outside Rome. There, the two passengers will board another plane, this one bound for Vienna, where German authorities will receive them and Mussolini's safety will be guaranteed.

When Skorzeny returns to Berlin, every Nazi leader wants to meet him. He receives the Knight's Cross of the Iron Cross—the highest military honor in the Reich—and is asked to tell the story of the rescue over and over again. And Hitler himself calls to thank him personally. "You have performed a military feat which will become part of history," he tells him. "You have given me back my friend Mussolini."

At last, after all the fanfare, it's time for Skorzeny to get back to what he was doing before he left for Italy. That means, among other things, training and overseeing missions to Iran. On top of all the hype surrounding the Mussolini rescue, one of the key takeaways—for the Nazi leadership and for Skorzeny himself—is a simple one: Special operations work. Small teams working in secret can often accomplish things that big armies cannot.

Skorzeny proved it.

And with the right elite team, he can prove it again.

28

Berlin, Germany

— LATE SEPTEMBER 1943 —

When and how do the Germans first learn that Tehran is a possible location for the Big Three summit?

There's no precise answer—no definitive record of when the Reich first obtained this information. There are only a few clues to invite speculation.

It's possible that Schellenberg's SD learns early on that Tehran is the likely location for the summit. After his meeting with Admiral Canaris, when the two intelligence chiefs discussed Hitler's desire for information about any pending Big Three conference, he certainly would have been making an effort to learn what he could by any means necessary.

After September 8, references to Tehran pepper the correspondence of the Big Three, as well as that of their high-level military and diplomatic staffs. And shortly after the Allied leaders first mention Tehran as a possible location, the SD's Near East division begins preparing a mission into the Tehran region, called Operation Norma. Few formal records exist regarding this mission, but there are two details about the staffing that are known and that are worthy of note.

The first is that the mission will be overseen by Roman Gamotha, Franz Mayr's former comrade, who fled Tehran after the Allied invasion. He had reappeared in Berlin earlier in the summer. Second, the mission's tactical training will be overseen by none other than Otto Skorzeny. Although Skorzeny's role within the SD is the same as it was before he rescued Mussolini, he's now a national hero whose name has appeared in newspapers all over the world. He's rubbed shoulders with the Reich's elite and has received some of the highest accolades possible within the Nazi Party. Any mission with Skorzeny's name on it has got to be important.

Schellenberg knows as well as anyone that the Axis

position in the war has diminished greatly in recent months. The daily Nazi propaganda won't say it, but the fact is that with Italy on the verge of surrendering to the Allies and the mighty Wehrmacht suffering a series of defeats against the Red Army on the Eastern Front, Hitler desperately needs a win.

As a result, when Schellenberg and the SD staff in Berlin first learn that Tehran is a possible location for the conference, it must seem like a stroke of extraordinary luck—one they plan on using to their advantage. The Allied leaders have just so happened to choose a city where Nazi spy agencies have spent considerable time and resources building up an intelligence infrastructure, thanks in large part to Franz Mayr.

But there's something Schellenberg doesn't know about Franz Mayr. This past month, Mayr's circumstances have changed dramatically—and it's a change that puts the SD's plans for Iran in jeopardy.

29

ONE MONTH EARLIER . . .

Tehran, Iran

— August 15, 1943 —

At 1:15 a.m. on August 15, British agents descend on a house in Tehran. They got the address from one of the men they arrested the night before, when they also apprehended Werner Rockstroh, the radio operator from Operation Franz. Not surprisingly, given the late hour, the ground floor of the building is in darkness.

After sneaking around, the agents find a staircase leading up to the second floor. There, they come across a man. According to agency files, "He was challenged and made no attempt to resist."

One of the British agents flicks on the light. The man's

description resembles one they've been given time and time again over the course of two years.

"Are you Franz Mayr?" the lead agent asks.

"Yes," the man says, as guns are pointed at him.

At last. They've caught the Nazi ringleader.

The agents spin Mayr around, pressing his face to the wall, but before they can arrest him, he crumples to the floor.

Franz Mayr, the undercover Nazi agent and leader of the underground resistance movement, has just fainted.

He's not out for long, and soon the British have him back in headquarters. Aside from cursing out the local Tehranis whom he believes sold him out, Mayr doesn't have much fight left in him. Perhaps, after living in hiding for so long, he is simply exhausted.

Within a few days, he has agreed to cooperate. He sits for interrogation. He stops fighting. He knows that this will be a long, grueling process, covering weeks and months, but it's not like he has a choice. His physical safety is now in the hands of his enemies. No doubt, there's little hope for a happy ending.

For years, this loyal Nazi lived a double life, ran an underground network of operatives, and served as the de facto leader of the pro-Nazi movement in Iran. Now, Franz Mayr is in custody and ready to answer any question.

30

SIX WEEKS LATER . . .

Washington, DC

— October 1, 1943 —

For months, there's been a flurry of correspondence between the three Allied leaders.

Now, in the wake of Stalin's agreement to a Big Three meeting before the end of the year, the flurry becomes a blizzard.

Stalin wants any meeting of the leaders to be preceded by a cabinet-level conference so the war planners and diplomats can iron out complicated issues in advance. It will also serve as a backup in case the Big Three conference doesn't happen.

After some back and forth, this is organized for

October 18, to be held in Moscow. The American Secretary of State, Cordell Hull, and the British Foreign Secretary, Anthony Eden, will attend, as will their Soviet counterpart, Vyacheslav Molotov.

For his part, Roosevelt plans to make the best possible use of this long journey across the globe. Specifically, he wants to meet with the Chinese leader, Chiang Kai-shek. As the country that has suffered more than any other in the face of Japanese aggression and imperialism, China has been a US ally from the beginning, and Roosevelt wants to shore up Chinese support for the next phase of the war in the Pacific.

The tricky thing is that the geopolitics of a meeting with Chiang are complicated. When the United States first forged its alliance with the UK and the USSR against the Axis powers, Stalin insisted that the Soviet Union maintain its own separate peace agreement with Japan. He needed every available soldier and weapon for his defense against the Nazis and had no interest in fighting the Japanese. As a result, the two nations agreed to a truce even while fighting on opposite sides of the larger war.

What this means now is that Stalin can't be present at any event also attended by Chiang, because that would signify that Stalin was taking sides in the conflict between

China and Japan—which Stalin has assured the Japanese he wouldn't do. To get around the issue, Roosevelt organizes a conference with Chiang in Cairo for early November, before the proposed Big Three meeting. Churchill will also join for part of it.

There's only one remaining obstacle for Roosevelt: the location.

Although Churchill accepted Tehran, he agrees to help Roosevelt try to persuade Stalin to meet somewhere else. Eritrea. Iraq. On board a ship in the Mediterranean Sea. The answer from Stalin is always the same. No.

"Unfortunately, not one of the places proposed by you for the meeting instead of Tehran is acceptable for me," he writes. He gives no alternatives.

Roosevelt keeps pushing. He suggests even more locations and expresses frustration that "I would have to travel six thousand miles and you would only have to travel six hundred miles from Russian territory." Stalin won't budge. It's Tehran or nowhere.

Why is Stalin being so stubborn? His stated reason, repeated multiple times, is that the Soviets have an offensive against the Germans planned for later in November, and he will need to be in constant contact with his military leaders during that time. Only in Tehran, he says, do the Soviets have secure and reliable communication lines directly to Moscow.

Stalin may be sincere in his focus on military affairs, but it's impossible for Roosevelt not to suspect that he is also trying to flex some power. Given his resentment for their long delay in opening a second front in Western Europe, he may be showing them that he gets to call the shots, too.

If Roosevelt won't travel to Tehran, Stalin finally says, the Soviets will send a high-level representative to meet him and Churchill anywhere they like while he himself stays in Moscow. Or, he suggests, they can wait and do the Big Three summit in the spring, when Soviet armies will not be as active.

For Roosevelt, this isn't a solution. After the recent string of Allied military successes, he believes they must seize the initiative. The time for the Big Three summit is not next spring—it's now. As for Molotov or another lower-level Soviet emissary coming in Stalin's place, that simply won't have the same global impact.

Stalin seems to be one of the most stubborn men on the planet. Roosevelt doesn't want to cave, but he doesn't have much choice. The Big Three meeting is simply too important, and right now all signs point to Tehran.

31

Washington, DC

— NOVEMBER 2, 1943 —

Whenever Mike Reilly, the head of the White House Secret Service, is summoned to speak to the President, it's usually bad news. Today is no exception.

As Reilly takes a seat, Roosevelt gets right to the point.

In three weeks' time, he has to get to Cairo. In Egypt. That's three thousand miles farther than their trip to Casablanca earlier in the year. On top of that, he tells Reilly, he "hopes to talk to Stalin" during this trip. And since Stalin can't come to Cairo, Roosevelt may have to go somewhere else even farther away.

To Reilly, it sounds like a logistical and security nightmare. But his job isn't to challenge the President's travel choices; his job is to keep everyone safe. It'll be up to him to plan the President's travel itinerary to Cairo and all the stops and stayovers along the way.

"Cordell Hull is in Moscow now," Roosevelt explains, referring to the Secretary of State, who is at the Moscow conference. "He is trying to make the arrangements for a meeting between Stalin and me." Roosevelt tells Reilly that Hull will be returning through Africa on his way back, so Reilly should go to Africa right now to meet him, learn from him what the latest itinerary will be, and start making preparations. "Whatever he has been able to arrange will be all right with me," the President says.

One thing Reilly and his staff know plenty about, especially after organizing the trip to Casablanca at the start of the year, is the danger that foreign air travel poses for the President. "Because the Boss couldn't use normal steps, it was necessary to build ramps wherever his plane was to land," Reilly later wrote, "and they were an absolute giveaway to any enemy agents."

For this reason, where possible, they will have to minimize the President's total number of flights. There's no way to avoid air travel once Roosevelt reaches Africa, but for the first part of the journey, they do have another option: the ocean. With the help of his military contacts, Reilly secures passage on board the battleship USS *Iowa* for the Commander in Chief's voyage across the Atlantic. Once the ship makes it to Algeria, Roosevelt will travel on to Cairo by plane.

Travel by sea is not without its own dangers—German U-boats stalk the ocean shipping lanes—but Reilly's team feels confident that, with an escort fleet, the mighty *Iowa* can fend off any Nazi subs.

As soon as these initial plans are in place, Reilly packs his bag. Having arranged with the State Department to meet Secretary Hull in Morocco, he embarks on a travel route using the next available military aircraft and pilots. The journey takes him from Washington, DC, to New York City, Cuba, Trinidad, Belém in Brazil, Dakar in French West Africa, and, finally, Morocco.

At Marrakech airport, a car is waiting for him, and when Reilly gets into the vehicle, he finds himself alone with Secretary of State Cordell Hull. Quickly, Reilly explains that the President asked him to confer with Hull to determine where, after Cairo, Roosevelt will travel to meet Stalin. By this point in time, Stalin still hasn't budged, and Roosevelt has finally agreed to the location.

"Well, it's Tehran, then," the Secretary of State tells him.

Reilly is one of the first people outside of Hull and the President himself to hear the location of the Big Three conference.

"Good luck, Mike," Hull tells him as they shake hands. "I'll tell the President I saw you."

Reilly's work in North Africa is just beginning. He'll now personally scout every step of Roosevelt's planned journey to establish security for both travel and lodging adequate for a US President during wartime. These preparations will take him to Oran, a city in Algeria, to Tunis, the capital of Tunisia, and to Cairo to prepare for the President's arrival there.

Then it's on to Tehran.

32

Lublin, Poland

— NOVEMBER 3, 1943 —

It starts with music.

At dawn, traditional German songs blare out from loudspeakers at the Majdanek concentration camp in Lublin, Poland. The sound of the music drowns out another sound: the thudding of boots hitting the ground as SS guards march through the camp.

An extra five hundred soldiers arrived the night before, and now, at 5 a.m., they march from building to building, rounding up the Jewish prisoners and forcing them into lines. Then they march the prisoners—many of them sick and emaciated—toward the outskirts of the camp. There are men, women, teenagers, small children, and older people.

When they see where they're going, a terrified wail rises above the music flooding the air. For the past several days, the prisoners have been digging a series of deep, zigzagging trenches around the camp perimeter. They were told that these were to house antiaircraft weapons. But the prisoners sensed that they were for something else—something terrible.

Now they realize that they were right.

As they approach the trenches, the guards organize the prisoners into groups of ten or fifteen. Anyone who tries to run or resist is beaten and pulled back in line—or simply shot.

The guards order them to strip naked. Then they push them, one by one, to the bottom of the trench and tell them to lie face down. The others watch and weep while a row of soldiers standing along the edge of the trench raise their weapons and shoot each prisoner in the back of the head.

The blaring music can't hide the gunshots or the screams.

It goes on like this all day, group after group, the trenches slowly filling with corpses.

This planned massacre was held today because it is

Erntefest, or "Harvest Festival," a traditional German holiday. Back in Germany, Reich leaders have encouraged citizens to celebrate the patriotic holiday with food, drink, and dancing. Similar mass killings are taking place at two smaller camps nearby—Trawniki and Poniatowa. By the end of the day, an estimated forty-two thousand Jewish prisoners will have been shot to death in the three camps. Some eighteen thousand are murdered here, in Majdanek.

There's something else behind the day's unspeakable carnage. Over the past few months, there have been multiple attempted insurgencies in the concentration camps. These were all unsuccessful and resulted in the executions of the prisoners involved. But a few German guards were injured, and a small number of Jewish prisoners escaped. Heinrich Himmler, the SS leader, decided that a swift, strong response was required. That is why he personally gave the order for today's slaughter.

Operation Harvest Festival will be counted as one of the worst single-day massacres of civilians during World War II. But apart from the sheer number of victims, there's nothing special about it. Majdanek is just one of thousands of death camps in the Nazi-occupied territories, and mass killings are happening every day—by starvation, by bullet, or in the gas chambers. As the German military falters against the Soviet Union and its Western Allies, the SS leaders are pushing harder and harder to complete the genocidal program of the Final Solution.

For a time, SS officials debate how Jewish children should be handled. Some officers and soldiers find it particularly difficult to shoot young children, or to beat them to death, or to watch them starve. In a meeting with Nazi leaders in October 1943, a month before Operation Harvest Festival, Himmler addresses these qualms:

> *I did not regard myself as justified in exterminating the men—that is to say, to kill them or have them killed—and to allow the avengers in the shape of the children to grow up for our sons and grandchildren. The difficult decision had to be taken to have this people disappear from the earth.*

Children, then, are not to be spared. In the trenches of Majdanek, and elsewhere, their corpses lie with those of the adults.

Operation Harvest Festival occurs at the same time that

the Moscow conference is taking place. The delegates at the conference are not aware of these particular massacres in the Polish death camps, but they do know that crimes against humanity are being carried out by the Nazi regime and its collaborators, and they have been drafting a declaration that is soon to be signed by Roosevelt, Churchill, and Stalin.

"The United Kingdom, the United States and the Soviet Union have received from many quarters evidence of atrocities, massacres and cold-blooded mass executions which are being perpetrated by Hitlerite forces in many of the countries they have overrun and from which they are now being steadily expelled," the statement begins.

The declaration will provide the framework for the later prosecution of former Nazi officials accused of war crimes. For now, though, it's just words on a sheet of paper. And words on paper can do nothing to stop the horrors taking place. While Allied diplomats and politicians meet around conference tables, innocent people, including children, are being slaughtered all over Eastern Europe in an ongoing campaign of mass murder and genocide.

It's not enough, then, for the Allies to achieve victory:

They must achieve it with the greatest possible urgency and speed. They must combine their resources and come up with a plan to strike back at the Nazi regime, crippling it in the only place that currently matters.

The battlefield.

33

The Atlantic Ocean

— NOVEMBER 14, 1943 —

Franklin Roosevelt loves the ocean.

He learned to sail as a child and practically grew up on boats. When, at the age of thirty-nine, he was stricken with the paralyzing disease of polio, the only way he could exercise was in water. The countless hours of physical therapy in ponds, lakes, and oceans enabled him to regain movement in his upper body. After his return to politics and public life, he spent almost every vacation on the waves.

Today, he's in his wheelchair, gazing out at the expanse of the Atlantic from the deck of the USS *Iowa*. They are several hundred miles from the nearest shore. At last, after so much planning, he's on his way to Cairo, and then it's on to Tehran. Standing behind him, as usual, is a Secret Service agent—one of Reilly's men. Also nearby is Admiral Ernest Joseph King, Commander in Chief of the US fleet and Chief of Naval Operations.

Roosevelt does some of his best thinking on the decks of boats, and right now there's a lot to think about. He capitulated to Stalin on Tehran. There's no other way to put it. He would have to make his peace with that. After Stalin refused to compromise, he had no choice, and whether Stalin was sincere in insisting on Tehran or engaging in a power play, it no longer matters. The important thing is this: The Big Three meeting is happening.

On November 8, Roosevelt wrote to Stalin and formally accepted Tehran as the location for the conference. He tried to give his message an inspirational note. "The whole world is watching for this meeting of the three of us," he wrote. "The fact that you and Churchill and I have got to know each other personally will have far-reaching effect on the good opinion within our three nations and will assist in the further disturbance of Nazi morale." Finally, he added, "I am greatly looking forward to a good talk with you."

Stalin's response, sent on November 10, was brief. "I thank you for your answer. Your plan concerning the organization of our meeting in Iran, I accept."

No high-minded words or shared principles.

Stalin is not the only Big Three partner who's been causing anxiety for Roosevelt. Churchill is once again losing his nerve about the cross-Channel attack. Invading the beaches of northern France carries enormous risk, and Churchill could end up presiding over a disaster, only a few miles from England's shores. "I now feel that the year 1944 is loaded with danger," he wrote to Roosevelt on October 27.

Ominously, Churchill suggested that he and his advisers were rethinking the entire strategy: "We have had prolonged discussions here about our existing plans for the campaign of 1944. On these the British Chiefs of Staff and War Cabinet are deeply concerned."

US military leaders are worried that Churchill and the British will once again delay, downgrade, or otherwise compromise Operation Overlord. Roosevelt will have to use Stalin's presence in Tehran to exert maximum pressure on Churchill to commit fully to the attack.

Suddenly, Roosevelt's train of thought is interrupted. The ship's officers have planned a demonstration of the

Iowa's awesome defensive firepower for his benefit. They launch a series of weather balloons to serve as targets, and soon the battleship's antiaircraft guns are blazing. The President, Admiral, and several dozen others watch from the deck as the ship's roughly one hundred gun turrets shoot down balloon after balloon. The few that drift out of range are taken down by a nearby destroyer serving as escort. It's an altogether impressive display, and the assembled spectators are in awe as they watch the firepower of the US Navy's finest ships.

Just then, the radio blares on the bridge. "Torpedo is coming your way!"

Must be part of the demonstration.

But the ship's senior officers look utterly worried.

"This is not a drill!" blares the voice over the loudspeakers. "Torpedo on the starboard beam!"

Alarm bells ring, and the air fills with the sound of crew members' feet pounding as they race to their battle stations. This is most definitely not a drill. A live torpedo is heading straight for the *Iowa*. And the President of the United States is sitting in his wheelchair on the starboard side of the bridge, unable to run.

Where did it come from? A Nazi U-boat, or some other enemy nearby? The answer is almost worse. It's one of their own. One of the escort ships, the destroyer USS *William D. Porter,* is participating in the demonstration for the President and was meant to discharge several harmless blank torpedoes for the *Iowa* to detect and intercept.

But there was a terrible mistake. The torpedomen on the destroyer failed to remove the explosive from one of the torpedoes. By the time the mistake is realized, the live torpedo is shooting through the water at over fifty miles per hour, heading straight toward the *Iowa* and President Roosevelt.

Captain John McCrea, the *Iowa*'s commanding officer, has one overwhelming reaction: turn the ship. By turning *toward* the coming torpedo, the battleship—so much longer than it is wide—makes for a much narrower target. As it turns, the ship creates a swell of waves that collide with the torpedo, causing it to detonate. The underwater explosion is felt on board even from a thousand yards away.

As for Roosevelt, the President is initially confused by the commotion, but once he grasps what has happened, and that he and his staff are not in harm's way, he asks to be wheeled to a rail on the bridge so he can watch.

The episode—an American destroyer shooting a live torpedo directly at a battleship carrying the President—will go down as one of the most embarrassing mistakes in the history of the US Navy. Immediately following the incident, the Navy orders the arrest of every officer and crew member aboard the *Porter* and sends the ship straight to nearby Bermuda for a full investigation.

When the crisis is past, Presidential adviser and Roosevelt's friend Harry Hopkins tries to lighten the mood by declaring that whoever shot the missile from the destroyer "must have been some damn Republican!" Still, for those whose job it is to keep the President safe, it's an unwelcome reminder of the perils of wartime travel with the Commander in Chief. Even here, in safe waters, surrounded by a massive US fleet, the President's life was put in danger.

34

Berlin, Germany

— NOVEMBER 4, 1943 —

The information sometimes comes so fast, it's hard to know what to do with it.

That's certainly true for the SD. Walter Schellenberg and his team are focused on trying to answer some simple questions. Will the Big Three ever have their long-rumored conference, and, if they do, when and where will it take place?

While it's not entirely clear what the SD knew about the Tehran summit or when they knew it, they certainly knew enough to keep them planning secret missions to Iran and to put Skorzeny in charge of those missions.

It's during this generally murky period that they get some unwelcome news.

Franz Mayr and the Operation Franz team are no longer responding to SD radio messages. On October 20, they find out why. Mayr has been arrested. That probably means that his network has been compromised and that others have been arrested, too, including the other members of Operation Franz.

Even worse, they find out that this happened over two months ago—in August. For eight weeks, they have been planning missions to Iran without knowing that they can no longer rely on the support of Mayr and his network. This is bad news.

However, a stroke of good luck is just around the corner—one that no one could have seen coming. Just days after learning about Mayr's arrest, Walter Schellenberg receives an urgent message from the office of Hitler's Foreign Minister, Joachim von Ribbentrop. They have come into possession of an extraordinary set of documents that they would like Schellenberg's agency to investigate.

The documents are actually photographs of documents: one photo per page. According to the source who delivered them, they're the confidential papers of the British Ambassador to Turkey, Sir Hughe Knatchbull-Hugessen.

Turkey is a neutral country in the war, but, because of its location next to Iran, it would be an obvious subject of conversation for any Allied conference in the region. This means that the British Ambassador would know about the proposed Big Three summit—and that he would be in possession of highly sensitive diplomatic documents.

At first, Schellenberg approaches the dossier of photos with skepticism. It really does seem too good to be true. Surely, it must be a hoax or an Allied trap. Yet as his team reviews the dossier, he is stunned by its contents. "I could see that we had here highly secret correspondence between the British Embassy in Ankara and the Foreign Office in London," he later recalled.

What's even more extraordinary is how the photographs arrived in Ribbentrop's office. The British Ambassador's personal servant, a Turkish man, took photographs of the documents when his boss was not home. He then approached German government contacts in Ankara and offered to sell them the documents for a large sum. The man is willing to continue taking photographs of the Ambassador's papers—so long as the Germans keep paying him.

They call him Cicero, after the Roman philosopher, because "his documents speak so eloquently."

By early November, they are receiving Cicero's intelligence on a regular basis. It gives Schellenberg access to the most sensitive Allied documents from Turkey, Iran, Iraq, and Russia—often within a few days. He has access to the conference planning almost in real time.

He finds out that Stalin is insisting on Tehran as the location for the conference.

And that Roosevelt is saying no.

Bit by bit, letter by letter, he's got a front-row seat.

Where before there was only murky intelligence, pieced together from confusing Allied intercepts, now there is immediacy and clarity. Franz Mayr's capture was a setback, to be sure, but good fortune has smiled on the SD.

Schellenberg knows they must take advantage of it.

But good luck can flow both ways. The Soviets are about to get an intelligence breakthrough, too.

In western Ukraine, the war and Nazi occupation have left the region completely devastated. It's now overseen by a mix of German soldiers, military officials, and SS administrators. One of the Nazi officers is a square-jawed young lieutenant named Paul Siebert. Handsome and outgoing, Siebert is popular and well respected by his fellow officers and soldiers. Unbeknownst to them, however, his name is not actually Paul Siebert. It's Nikolai Kuznetsov.

And if this name doesn't sound German, that's because it isn't.

Kuznetsov is an undercover Soviet spy. With his Nordic appearance and flawless German, it's nearly impossible to tell that he's Russian, working undercover. Operating under different aliases, Kuznetsov has had a hand in multiple assassination plots against high-ranking Nazi officials in the Ukrainian cities of Lviv and Rivne. By some accounts, he personally pulled the trigger on a few of them. Every day, he risks his life gathering information about Nazi operations in the region, then sending it to his superiors in Moscow.

On this cold night, probably in early November, Kuznetsov, aka Siebert, is having drinks with a German special operations officer named Hans Ulrich von Ortel. Kuznetsov recently befriended von Ortel, just as he's befriended many other German officers and soldiers. He notices that the more von Ortel drinks, the more he talks. For a spy, this makes for a promising evening.

Sure enough, as Kuznetsov pours more and more cognac, von Ortel starts bragging. He says he's part of a team planning a top secret mission, the leader of which is none other than Otto Skorzeny, the special operations mastermind who led the mission to rescue Mussolini. He won't say anything more.

Then Kuznetsov remembers that von Ortel mentioned he needed a loan, so he tells him that he has access to some funds via a patriotic German who will grant him a loan. This comment generates some trust, as intended, and, more importantly, it causes von Ortel to slip up. "I'll repay you," he says, "in Persian rugs."

It's a tiny detail, but this throwaway comment contains a major hint about the mission's destination. It must be in Iran. As always, Kuznetsov makes sure to report the details of his conversation to Moscow. He might not know what to make of von Ortel's comment, but the experts back at headquarters are very interested in it.

A Nazi special operations mission, to Iran, led by Otto Skorzeny, with the training taking place in the weeks before the Big Three conference.

A coincidence? It doesn't seem likely.

35

Cairo, Egypt

— NOVEMBER 23, 1943 —

Mike Reilly is on another plane.

He's been on a lot of planes in the past two weeks—almost too many to count. He's also been on quite a few boats, trains, trucks, and jeeps. He's been in Algeria, Tunisia, Egypt, Iraq, and Iran—all scouting trips for the President's travels.

As soon as the USS *Iowa* docked in the port of Oran in Algeria, Reilly joined the President and traveled by plane with him to Cairo, where he was to meet Churchill and Chiang Kai-shek. During his earlier scouting trip, Reilly had found Cairo to be a city "seething with unrest," including violent demonstrations in front of the British and French embassies. According to his sources, the city was "filled with Axis spies."

Every possible precaution had to be taken to secure the conference. Reilly ordered a barbed wire entanglement be built to surround the entirety of the district where the meetings were to be held. American and British troops were posted around the Ambassador's compound where Roosevelt and much of the US delegation would be staying. The local waitstaff and groundskeeping staff were replaced with Americans for the duration of the event. Were this not done, an enemy assassin could end up being the one serving lunch to the delegates.

The US military also got involved. "The air raid defense system was reinforced with antiaircraft batteries and reconnaissance fighter planes," Reilly later recalled. Because intelligence photos of the nearby island of Crete showed the presence of German aircraft, US military planes bombed the island "before and during the time the President was in Cairo."

Finally, an armed team of Reilly's agents were on hand for every moment of the event. They were tasked with protecting the President and the US delegation, and they coordinated their efforts with the British and Chinese security teams who were also trying to keep their people safe.

With his team on duty and the location secure, Reilly headed for his next plane.

Now he is bound for Tehran. If all goes according to plan, the President will be traveling there in four days' time, as soon as the Cairo conference concludes. Reilly needs to get there first to prepare.

It's not his first trip to Tehran. He was there a week earlier to check the airfields and the roads to the city. Now he wants to inspect the city itself, plus the President's lodgings and the conference site. At the airport, he meets his Russian counterpart: General Dmitri Arkadiev of the NKVD. Reilly and Arkadiev will be sharing responsibility for the safety of the Allied leaders for the duration of the conference.

Reilly's first priority is to inspect the American legation on the southern outskirts of the city, where Roosevelt is to stay. Its most notable feature is its distant location—roughly a mile and a half across the city from the British and Soviet embassies, where Churchill and Stalin will be staying and where most of the meetings will take place. Roosevelt has made clear to Reilly that he wants to stay on American turf, to maintain his independence, but Reilly doesn't like the fact that the President will have to travel back and forth such a long way each day.

The next task is to inspect the British and Soviet embassies. Unlike the isolated American legation, the two embassies stand side by side in the center of the city, both surrounded by high walls. A narrow street separates the two compounds, which could easily be walled off to keep people away.

While Reilly is touring the Soviet embassy, Arkadiev pulls him aside. The General has a grave look on his face, which Reilly reads instantly as bad news. He's not wrong. According to Arkadiev, "the Germans [have] dropped parachutists in the Russian-occupied area near Tehran." Even worse, at least some of them were dropped yesterday. Arkadiev tells Reilly that the Soviet forces have not caught any of the Germans, who, they suspect, are now hiding in the mountains.

Reilly knows it can't get much worse. "The German parachutists could have been dropped for only one of two reasons," he later recalled. Either to sabotage the railroad that transports American supplies from the Persian Gulf to the Caspian Sea, or to assassinate the Allied leaders. If it's to sabotage a railroad, then why would the German parachutists be arriving now, within a day or two of the Big

Three's arrival? That seems a very unlikely coincidence. The more realistic—and terrifying—possibility is that the Germans know about the conference.

They need to assume the worst.

The two security experts spring into action. "We extended the protected area around the legations and doubled the guards," Reilly recalled. From that moment forward, "Russian, British and American Secret Service agents and intelligence officers combed Tehran, looking for the parachutists."

But in a city of three-quarters of a million people, with the added chaos of a major international summit taking place, how could they possibly locate and identify a few enemy agents?

It's not like the German parachutists are going to waltz through the city gates wearing Nazi uniforms. They'll find a way to blend in. To infiltrate.

And if they do that, they might already be here in Tehran, closer than anyone realizes.

36

Berlin, Germany

— NOVEMBER 1943 —

It's a one-of-a-kind opportunity.

For at least a few days, the three Allied leaders will be in the same city, in the same room—sometimes eating at the same table. When they're photographed together, it might even be in a public location. For Nazi special forces, there'll never be a better chance to hurt them all at once. The only question is, how do they get close enough to do it?

Given the nature of the event, it's easy to predict where the three leaders are staying: at their countries' respective embassies or legations. That's a starting point.

Of course, the Allies are aware that the enemy knows this, so they'll guard them like military fortresses. Any frontal assault on the individual compounds would be foolish. Better to find a subtle way in.

A simple map of the city reveals something important about the three countries' buildings. While the Soviet and British embassies are in the center of the city and next door to each other, the American legation is on the outskirts, isolated. That might not change the level of protection, but it does mean that once the meetings start, either the American President is going to have to travel through the city to meet the other two, or the other two will be traveling to the American President. Sure, there's the possibility that all three would meet at some neutral location, but then all three would be forced to travel through the streets.

In the compounds, they're safe. When they're traveling, they're exposed.

That's opportunity number one.

With a deeper knowledge of the city, which the Nazi intelligence services certainly have, there's a second opportunity. For each of the country's buildings, in addition to the ground-level doors and entrances, there's a network of underground tunnels. It's designed that way for the water. As most visitors to Tehran know, the city's supply of drinking water is unsafe for outsiders. In fact, it's not safe for locals, either. Residents usually draw their water from a source connected to the city's uneven sewer system, and that water is notoriously contaminated by bacteria from human and animal waste. It's even worse for Westerners, who are particularly vulnerable. Typhoid fever—the disease that claimed Karl Korel—is just one of many maladies that are rife.

Back when the Allies invaded and took over Tehran, they needed a solution to this problem. Instead of relying on imported bottled water or risking the local stuff, they set up a system to draw clean mountain water from outside the city, to those places where Russian, British, and American officials need it.

Hence the tunnels.

In those tunnels, the water flows directly to the three countries' diplomatic headquarters—the Russian embassy, the British embassy, and the American legation—as well as to the local US Army Command compound.

So, yes, a direct assault on one of the compounds might be doomed to fail.

But a surprise attack through one of the underground water tunnels? That's a different story.

To this day, it is unclear whether the German

intelligence agencies had their agents scout the tunnels, or whether they had maps or schematics to them. But the Germans most definitely knew that the tunnels existed and that humans traversed them.

Which leaves the big question: When would Roosevelt, Churchill, and Stalin all be together? Unless you know when to strike, there's no way to take down all three at once. The tricky part is, in the days before the summit, the Allies' itinerary of meetings still hasn't been set, and once it's finalized, it'll be top secret. Making things even harder, each meeting has a different configuration of people. Only a few have all three leaders, and most of them only include diplomats or Generals, with no leaders at all.

For any potential assassin, trying to determine the exact right day and time is confounding. Yet even a novice enemy intelligence officer would notice that a particular date of note happens to fall during the conference.

November 30, 1943. Winston Churchill's birthday.

His sixty-ninth, to be exact.

Whenever there's an international summit, there's the inevitable long, elaborate dinner where the leaders and attendees gather to socialize after their long day of meetings. These dinners don't necessarily take place every night, but the fact that Winston Churchill's birthday happens to fall in the middle of the conference?

It's a pretty good bet that all three will be in the same room at the same time.

If so, Winston Churchill could be in for a real birthday surprise.

37

Tehran, Iran

— NOVEMBER 27, 1943 —

Churchill doesn't like what he sees.

The British entourage left Cairo a few hours before the Americans, and when they arrive at Tehran's Gale Morghe airfield at 11 a.m., they head straight for the city. If all goes according to plan, the Big Three meeting will take place tomorrow afternoon.

Churchill is in the back of a car in a long line of vehicles, all of them driving on the desert road toward downtown Tehran. It's here that he starts to feel uneasy.

"As we approached the city, the road was lined with Persian cavalrymen every fifty yards for at least three miles," he later wrote. "It was clearly shown to any evil people that somebody of consequence was coming, and which way."

As Churchill's car approaches the city, large crowds start to gather. Anyone in the crowd might pose a danger, and there is no apparent means to prevent or act against that danger. In the event of an incident, the Iranian cavalrymen marking out the route would be able to provide no protection at all.

The vehicle slowly makes its way through the streets, where the problem only gets worse. Soon the crowds are "four or five deep." When the car stops at intersections, the onlookers press to within a few feet of the vehicle. Churchill is appalled. "There was no kind of defense at all against two or three determined men with pistols or a bomb." No one *seems* unfriendly—"I grinned at the crowd, and on the whole they grinned at me," as Churchill put it—but it would have been easily possible for a hostile enemy agent to be hidden among them.

By the time Churchill arrives at the British embassy, he is deeply unnerved.

The British and the Americans are entering a foreign and faraway city that they didn't choose to come to. On top of that, the Iranian people once had sympathies toward the Germans in the war, and many do not like the Allied occupation. There's an active pro-German underground movement in the city and evidence of local Nazi agents operating there.

To make matters worse, the local government has provided little in the way of security, leaving the Allied visitors to fend for themselves. Winston Churchill is not a stupid man. He's been in Tehran for barely an hour, and what he's feeling more than anything else is that he's in danger.

38

Tehran, Iran

— THE SAME AFTERNOON —

Later that day, at 3 p.m., President Roosevelt's plane arrives.

Protected by a large military escort, Roosevelt and his entourage drive from the airport to the American legation on the southern outskirts of the city. Once the President is settled—and safe—it's time for Reilly to get an update from the NKVD.

He hasn't told anyone in the President's circle about the German parachutists yet. It's too uncertain—better not to alarm everyone. At the Soviet embassy, he finally gets some good news. The NKVD chief tells him that Soviet agents have "captured some of the parachutists." They've also learned some more details, namely that "thirty-eight Nazis had been dropped around Tehran."

"Are you sure it was thirty-eight?" Reilly asks, trying to make a joke about the precision of the number.

"Very sure," the Soviet spy chief replies calmly. "We examined the men we caught most thoroughly."

"The way he said it made me happy I had not been present when the Nazis were questioned," Reilly later wrote.

Reilly might not have wanted to know what interrogation techniques the Russians used on the captured Nazis, but he certainly did want to know what they found out.

The examinations "disclosed that there were at least six German paratroopers loose in the vicinity with a radio transmitter," the Russian tells him.

Thirty-two Germans captured. Six still on the loose, and a radio by which they might be communicating with their handlers back in Berlin.

The Soviet security forces seem to be handling the situation well, but, even so, clear danger remains. Six Nazis might not be able to launch an assault on the Big Three compounds directly, given the huge security details that the American, British, and Soviets have put in place. But that's not how they would operate—even with a larger number of commandos. More likely, an assassin would sneak in. No matter how tight the security, there will be moments when Roosevelt, Churchill, and Stalin will be exposed.

All three need to travel by car through Tehran.

All three need to be in contact with local workers or staff.

All it would take is one gunman blending into a crowded street, one sniper finding the right rooftop, or one disguised German agent somehow infiltrating one of the facilities. Capture all the parachutists you want. If one gets through, none of that matters.

So, what should the Americans do? The NKVD chief tells Reilly what the Russians think they should do. Stalin would like "for the President to move from the isolated American legation to either the British or the Russian embassy, which were side by side in the heart of town and were both heavily walled."

Reilly likes the idea—it's the smart choice. The trouble is, the President has already told him that he wants to stay at the American legation. Reilly doesn't have the authority to make a decision that overrules the President's wishes.

As it turns out, someone else is about to make the decision for him.

39

Tehran, Iran

— THE SAME EVENING —

Averell Harriman, US Ambassador to the Soviet Union, is also making the rounds. He has been to the American legation, the Russian embassy, and the British embassy.

Finally, just before midnight, he arrives back at the US Army compound, where he himself is staying. He's looking forward to a few hours' sleep before the long and difficult day ahead.

Just as he's settling in for the night, he receives a message from the Soviet Foreign Minister, Vyacheslav Molotov. Harriman already met at length with Molotov earlier that afternoon. He's got no idea why the Russian would need to contact him again. But the message says that Molotov needs to see him in person now—as in *right now*—at the Soviet embassy. He has also requested that the British Ambassador, Archibald Clark Kerr, join them.

So much for sleep.

It's very late when the two Ambassadors arrive, with their security escorts, at the walled Soviet embassy compound. They still have no idea why Molotov has called them. Molotov tells them that he has "received bad news . . . German agents in Tehran [have] learned of Roosevelt's presence in the city," and they are planning a "demonstration."

Harriman asks him to explain. Molotov looks at them both. "There might be an assassination attempt," he says.

An assassination attempt. By German agents. And they're learning about it in the early hours of the day before the conference is set to begin.

Unbeknownst to Harriman and Kerr, this is what Mike Reilly learned earlier from General Arkadiev and the NKVD.

"Even if it failed," Molotov continues, an attempt "would certainly lead to shooting and might result in the killing of innocent bystanders." Such an incident would create "a most unfortunate scandal for the Allies, which would be bound to be exploited by the Nazi propaganda machine."

Naturally, the Ambassadors want every piece of information they can get from the Soviets. Harriman later recalled, "I pressed him within the limits of civility for details." But Molotov, a foreign minister and not an intelligence officer, doesn't have much more to share. It was Stalin who asked him to personally share this information.

So, does Stalin have a plan? He certainly has a suggestion. To avoid danger, rather than stay at the American legation, Roosevelt should move to the Soviet embassy.

The Soviet compound is large, with plenty of room. The British will be right next door. None of the leaders will have to drive through the Tehran streets in broad daylight to meet each other.

Molotov gives Harriman a tour of the compound and shows him a villa where Roosevelt and his top staff could stay and still remain independent. The Soviets have already started working on the plumbing and are making other arrangements in the event that the President accepts.

Harriman looks around the villa. "Although the furnishings were overelaborate and ugly," he later recalled, "the quarters looked comfortable enough."

Thanking Molotov for the information, Harriman says

goodbye to the British Ambassador, then travels back to the US military compound, where he arranges to speak to its commander, General Donald Connolly, and Mike Reilly. Harriman and Reilly both share with Connolly the conversations they had with the Soviets.

The stories match up.

From there, the three men come up with a plan.

It starts with this: Tomorrow morning, they meet with Roosevelt—and tell the President his life is in danger.

40

Tehran, Iran

— NOVEMBER 28, 1943 —

It's an emergency meeting. The following morning, at 9:30, Franklin Delano Roosevelt, the President of the United States, sits in his quarters at the US legation, facing the members of his military staff and security team. In an adjacent room, other advisers are talking hurriedly to one another and pacing up and down. They're all trying to digest what they've just heard from the Soviets: The Big Three are in danger.

Ambassador Harriman does most of the talking, but the others contribute, too.

Stalin and Molotov, Harriman says, want to convey

that Tehran is full of Axis sympathizers and that an "unhappy" incident might occur to any of the heads of state driving through the city to reach one another. Specifically, Russian intelligence has discovered that the Germans have dropped paratroopers near the city. While most have been arrested, some are still at large. Stalin is scheduled to visit the American legation later this afternoon for an initial greeting, with Churchill arriving soon after. This means that "the risk of assassination of Mr. Churchill and Marshal Stalin while coming to visit the President [is] very real."

Harriman goes on to tell Roosevelt that the Russians have proposed for him to move his quarters to the Russian embassy to "bring the three heads of state so close together that there would be no need for any of them to drive about town." He adds that he personally inspected the quarters offered by the Russians and found them acceptable.

His final point is that whatever decision they make doesn't just affect the safety of the American President. As Harriman puts it, if they don't move to the Russian compound, "we would be responsible for any injury that Marshal Stalin might suffer in driving through the town to consult with President Roosevelt."

Roosevelt wants to know what the others think.

Admiral Wilson Brown doesn't like deferring so quickly to Stalin's proposal. He points out that "it was Stalin who suggested Tehran and why was he objecting now to security?" It's a fair point.

There's one other person Roosevelt wants to hear from: Mike Reilly.

Reilly says that he "is in full agreement" that Roosevelt should move from the American legation. With Nazi agents lurking in the city, "Stalin and Churchill would be subjected to unnecessary danger when they came to visit him," and Russian NKVD men felt that Roosevelt was risking "not only his life but theirs by living outside of town."

Reilly feels the need to clarify this last point: "If anything [happens] to the President of the United States, we in the Secret Service would be deeply embarrassed, but the Russian Secret Service men would be dead before nightfall."

It's a hell of a detail.

In the end, it's Roosevelt's call.

"Do you care which embassy I move to?" he asks Reilly.

"Not much difference, sir," Reilly answers.

Roosevelt takes a moment to think. Despite the alarming news he has just heard, he's not really focused on his personal safety—that's the job of his security staff and of the US military. Mostly, he's thinking about his master strategy for the conference. The fact is that this Nazi assassination plot has given him a nice opportunity.

"All right. It's the Russian, then," he says.

Because the threat of an assassination attempt is "very real," somehow they need to get Roosevelt and his entire entourage to the other side of town without anyone knowing about it.

The good thing is, Mike Reilly already has a plan.

41

How do you guarantee the safety of a President in a large, loud, conspicuous motorcade as it rolls through the center of a densely packed city?

The simple answer is, you can't.

A motorcade is too big to keep secret, and they cannot guarantee the President's safety if he's part of it.

"I had no stomach for sending him through the crowded streets of Tehran," Reilly later recalled. "It would have been a tough enough job normally, but with six Nazi paratroopers around somewhere it was a real headache."

So where does that leave him? With one of the best weapons in the Secret Service arsenal. Deception. The single best way to keep the President safe is to make people look for him in a place where he isn't.

"We lined the entire route with soldiers, shoulder to shoulder. We set up the standard cavalcade with the gun-laden jeeps fore and aft, and it traveled slowly along the streets guarded by soldiers," Reilly later described.

The entourage proceeds slowly into the city, the Presidential sedan at the center of it all. In no time, the crowds come running. Everyone's excited to see the President of the United States. The catch is, Roosevelt isn't anywhere near the procession.

"As soon as the cavalcade left the American legation," Reilly later explained, "we bundled the President into another car [and] put a jeep in front of him." The two nondescript vehicles head out in a different direction from the motorcade and then go "tearing through the ancient side streets of Tehran."

Meanwhile, the dummy cavalcade wends its way slowly through the main streets. Onlookers and soldiers crane their necks to get a glimpse of one of the most powerful men in the world. Who they're seeing is Bob Holmes, the

Secret Service agent who gamely accepted the role as the President's body double. Holmes is prepared to literally take a bullet should an assassin get off a good shot.

Three men accompany the real President: Admiral Leahy of the Navy, Major Boettiger of the Army, and Roosevelt's trusted friend and adviser, Harry Hopkins. They'll protect the President should they run into any trouble.

True to his nature, Roosevelt isn't worried for his own safety. In fact, he enjoys the high drama, ducking down to avoid being seen while the two vehicles race through the winding backstreets of the city. "The Boss . . . was vastly amused by the dummy cavalcade trick and the other cops-and-robbers stuff," Reilly later put it. "I was glad it amused him, because it did not amuse me much."

Indeed, the entire episode is highly stressful for Reilly and the Secret Service. Playing this elaborate trick might have been the safest option available to them, but that doesn't mean they're out of danger. If the Nazis figure out the truth, or stumble on the little two-car convoy, the President will be beyond vulnerable. And if the Nazis fall for the trap and take aim at the dummy cavalcade, there will be victims there as well—including Reilly's agent Bob Holmes. Holmes may be wearing a bulletproof vest, but a well-aimed bullet could still take his life.

It's not until armed guards wave Roosevelt's sedan through the gate of the heavily guarded Soviet embassy and Reilly is informed of the President's safe arrival that he can finally breathe a sigh of relief.

On day one of the conference at least, they've kept the President safe.

Now the real adventure begins.

42

Roosevelt made careful arrangements to meet Stalin informally, one-on-one, before Churchill arrived.

After Soviet aides show him and his staff to the villa where they'll be staying, he isn't left with much time to prepare. Just a few minutes later, Mike Reilly receives word that Stalin is on his way.

"I'll talk to him in the sitting room, Mike," Roosevelt says. "Stall him a second while I get ready."

The Americans waiting outside the villa are the first to see Stalin emerge from the main embassy building, flanked by his security detail, and walk down a tree-lined path toward the villa. After a year of buildup and preparation, this is what everyone has been waiting for.

"Seeing him for the first time was indeed a shock," Reilly later wrote. Stalin's official portrait is well known all over the world, and it is strange to see a somewhat ordinary-looking man walking toward them. At five foot four, he is also shorter than everyone else present—especially the Russian guards who tower over him.

"His hair was white, and his yellowish face was pock-marked," Major John Bates, one of Roosevelt's military escorts, notices. Stalin's left arm was slightly deformed, and his gait was a little bit awkward. Yet there was a mysterious aura around him that commanded a mix of fear and respect.

"He was a small man, indeed," Reilly remembered, "but there was something about him that made him look awfully big."

The Americans open the door to the villa for Stalin to enter. Roosevelt, waiting in his wheelchair, watches as Stalin "sort of amble[s] across the room" and, with a big grin under his trademark mustache, reaches down to shake his hand.

"At last!" Roosevelt says, also grinning. "I am glad to see you. I have tried for a long time to bring this about."

Stalin returns the greeting, offering Roosevelt a Russian cigarette. Stalin has done his homework—he knows the President likes to smoke.

Whenever he meets someone new, Roosevelt often likes to open with something lighthearted. Pointing to a photograph on the wall of Stalin smoking a pipe, FDR suggests that, during the conference, they should get a photograph of the three Allied leaders: Stalin with his pipe, Churchill with his trademark cigar, and Roosevelt with his cigarette and filter holder.

Stalin lets out a chuckle.

Soon, everyone exits the room except for the two leaders and their interpreters.

Roosevelt asks about progress on the Eastern Front, and they talk about shipping delays, France, the latest developments in China. It's all quite informal—none of it touching on the topics they both know will be covered during the formal sessions. Roosevelt's purpose for this meeting is to establish a rapport with Stalin and to get a sense of his personality. That way, during the upcoming meetings, he will be able to anticipate the Russian's rhythms and manner of speaking.

He also wants to establish that he's an independent entity: that he and Stalin can collaborate independently of

Churchill should the need arise. With this goal accomplished, the Big Three summit can officially begin. The two leaders leave the villa—accompanied, as always, by their armed security teams—and head toward the embassy building for the first session, which is scheduled for 4 p.m.

The British arrive from the opposite direction. Soon, the three groups are mingling in the entryway to the conference hall. Churchill is having a rough day. He caught a cold in Cairo, and now he has a sore throat that makes it difficult to speak. In a bad mood to begin with, he is even more agitated that Roosevelt declined his invitation to meet over lunch. All day, the President's entire focus has been on Stalin.

Once the small talk is done and the participants are seated around the conference table, each leader makes introductory remarks.

Stalin speaks in a matter-of-fact tone. "I take pleasure in welcoming those present . . . Now let us get down to business."

43

Roosevelt begins the session with a survey of America's position in the war. He describes the recent advances of US forces in the Pacific theater and gives an update on American arms production and shipping.

Then, and very quickly, he gets to the subject that everyone at the table knows is the most important topic under discussion.

Operation Overlord.

The cross-Channel attack has almost torn apart this alliance. It's also what everyone knows will determine the course of the war. For this reason, Roosevelt has a definite preplanned strategy for this conference: gain Stalin's trust and put pressure on Churchill.

He starts by making it clear that a cross-Channel attack from England into northern France has been the centerpiece of their war planning and that "an immense expedition . . . had been set . . . for May 1, 1944." There are questions about what to do with the Anglo-American forces after the fall of Rome, which they expect to occur in January. He's heard some ideas from Churchill about how these forces might be utilized for future missions in the Mediterranean, but that would draw resources from and delay the schedule for the cross-Channel attack:

> We cannot do everything we would like to do in the Mediterranean and also from the United Kingdom . . . If we were to conduct any large expedition in the Mediterranean, it would be necessary to give up this important cross-Channel operation, and certain contemplated operations in the Mediterranean might result in a delay in Overlord for one month or two or three.

The goal, Roosevelt says, is that "he and the Prime Minister had desired to ascertain the views of Marshal Stalin on this point." This is Roosevelt lobbing a massive softball to Stalin, and the Soviet leader is ready to swing.

"The best method in the Soviet opinion," Stalin replies, repeating what he always says, is "getting at the heart of Germany with an attack through northern or northwestern France." He acknowledges that the Mediterranean operations have been "of great importance in order to produce freedom of navigation," but he believes that "now they are of no further great importance as regards the defeat of Germany."

Just like that, Stalin—with a little help from Roosevelt—has put Churchill on the defensive.

Now it's Churchill's turn to speak. He begins by saying he wants to make it clear that he has "long agreed with the United States that an invasion of North and Northwestern France across the Channel should be undertaken." He has been considering "what could be done with forces in the Mediterranean area during this period to bring the greatest pressure to bear on the enemy." He's interested in various operations east of the Mediterranean—in Greece and the Balkans—and admits that "some of the operations which had been discussed might involve a delay of some two months in Overlord."

To Stalin, this sounds like a repeat of everything he's been hearing for the past two years. They say they're in for the mission, then they delay. He demands now that "Overlord be accepted as a basis for operations in 1944 and other operations should be considered as diversionary." If they're worried about Anglo-American forces in Italy having nothing to do, they could organize a supplementary attack on southern France just before the cross-Channel attack so they would be supporting Overlord rather than delaying it.

As the session continues, the issue remains unresolved. Even when they move on to other subjects, Overlord looms over everything. Until they're in sync on this key matter, there can be no unity.

The meeting ends at 7:20 p.m., and the Big Three gather again at 8:00 p.m. for the first dinner of the summit. It's hosted by the Americans, with a menu of steak and potatoes. During dinner, Roosevelt feels queasy and excuses himself, but once he's settled back at his villa, he soon feels better.

It's been a momentous day. He's learned about a Nazi

assassination plot, raced through the streets of Tehran huddled in the back of a car, met Soviet leader Joseph Stalin for the first time, and had a lively first meeting at the summit he's been anticipating for over a year. Regarding the conference itself, Roosevelt feels good about his strategy. He formed the rapport with Stalin that he wanted, and his plan to team up with the Soviet leader against Churchill regarding Operation Overlord seems to be working.

Now, at the end of a long day, he can finally relax and talk everything through with his most trusted friends and advisers.

The trouble is, those trusted friends and advisers are not the only ones listening. Hidden in the room's carpets, walls, and furniture are tiny microphones. And as the President and his team talk, someone is recording every word.

44

The weeks leading up to the summit were a busy time for any NKVD agents based in Tehran. First, there was a crackdown on Nazis in the city, with a sweep of arrests. Exact numbers vary, but the Russians brought in approximately two to three hundred local Nazi sympathizers.

Gevork Vartanian and his Light Cavalry comrades raced around the city on their bikes for "fourteen or sixteen hours per day," he later remembered, following suspects, tracking down leads, and sharing information. The British did the same. The two sides didn't always cooperate, but in the lead-up to the conference, Vartanian and the others were given some big news: British intelligence had captured Franz Mayr, the German spy and leader of the pro-Nazi movement in Tehran.

Like many on the Soviet side, Vartanian felt a pang of jealousy when he heard that the British had captured Mayr—"We wanted to get him first!" But there was still plenty for them to do. Rumors had spread, based on intelligence from a source in Ukraine, that the Germans were planning some sort of action at the conference, and there were more rumors of mysterious German parachute drops in and around the city.

The search now narrowed to the most important group of all: six Nazi agents with a radio and "loaded with weapons."

The NKVD tracked their landing and followed them to Tehran, where pro-German associates "had readied a villa for their stay."

Now the Russians had a decision to make. Should they arrest the six agents immediately or continue to observe them from a distance?

They decided to hold back.

The Light Cavalry would follow the Germans' every move.

"While we were watching the group, we established that they had contacted Berlin by radio," Vartanian recalled. Even better, "[we] recorded their communication."

When they decrypt these radio messages, the Soviets learn that the Germans are "preparing to land a second group of subversives for a terrorist act." Why does the NKVD think the second team is coming? Undoubtedly, it is for "the assassination or abduction of the Big Three." The Allies' worst fears come true.

The radio decrypts also give the NKVD a key new detail. "The second group was supposed to be led by Skorzeny himself," Vartanian said.

The NKVD must decide what to do. They could continue to monitor these agents, allowing the mission to proceed. This would give them the opportunity to capture or kill the action team when it arrives.

Or they could storm the villa now and shut down the operation.

Either way, time is short. The Allied conference has already begun.

45

— NOVEMBER 29, 1943 —

Churchill still has a cold.

Plus, on the second morning of the conference, he's frustrated. Day one didn't go as well as he'd hoped. He wants to talk to Roosevelt, frankly and confidentially, like they've always done. For two years, they've confronted every challenge together. Now, at this critical moment, there's a distance between them. Again, he invites Roosevelt to lunch so they can get aligned before they join Stalin in the afternoon. But again, just like the day before, Roosevelt declines his invitation. It's almost like he's worried that Stalin will hear about them meeting and think that he and Churchill are colluding against him.

The Prime Minister is savvy enough to comprehend Roosevelt's motives, but that doesn't ease the sting. When Ambassador Harriman declines the lunch invitation on the President's behalf, Churchill understands, but has a message:

> I shall insist on one thing: that I be host at dinner tomorrow evening. I think I have one or two claims to precedence. To begin with, I come first both in seniority and alphabetically. In the second place, I represent the longest established of the three governments. And, in the third place, it's my birthday.

A birthday party. It'll be the perfect send-off.

Later that day, the Big Three gather on the front portico of the Soviet embassy, where American, British, and Soviet war photographers are waiting. They sit on three adjacent chairs at the top of the steps. It's a moment captured for the ages: the three Allied leaders meeting for the first time. In a few days, when the conference is officially made known to the public, the photographs will be seen around the world. If Churchill's face bears something of a scowl in most of the photographs, it might be because he knows he's headed for a tough afternoon.

Roosevelt and Stalin are aligned on the issue they all

Allied leaders Joseph Stalin, Franklin Roosevelt, and Winston Churchill, aka the Big Three, sit for photographs outside the Soviet embassy in Tehran, Iran, on November 29, 1943. (Library of Congress)

know will once again dominate the afternoon's session: Operation Overlord, the cross-Channel attack. Churchill and his team come ready for a fight. They insist that additional operations east of the Mediterranean will have real value and that they only want flexibility on the date of the cross-Channel attack—maybe to extend it to July.

Stalin won't have it. Right away, he declares that Overlord is "the most important and nothing should be done to distract attention from that operation."

Roosevelt agrees with Stalin.

From there, the pile-on continues, with Roosevelt and Stalin insisting that the date be fixed for the following spring. Churchill and his team keep fighting. For hours, they approach the topic from various directions. Everyone's frustrated, and the argument grows heated. Roosevelt suggests they adjourn.

When they reconvene, for cocktails and dinner hosted by the Soviets, the tension hangs in the air. Churchill's mood remains sour. He's losing the argument, and he knows it. During dinner, the leaders discuss subjects other than Overlord, but, as Harriman later recalled, even on these topics, "Stalin kept needling Churchill without mercy."

The Soviet leader speaks softly but in a biting tone that

always seems aimed at the British Prime Minister. According to Harriman, "Several times through the evening [Stalin] plainly [implies] that the Prime Minister [is] nursing some secret affection for the Germans."

The bad feeling reaches a pinnacle as they discuss the possible fate of postwar Germany. Stalin worries that even a defeated Germany "would rise again within 15 or 20 years" unless the Allies take tough measures to contain it. Using some very Russian humor, he suggests, as a possible solution, "that some 50,000 or possibly 100,000 German military officers should be liquidated."

Churchill doesn't see Stalin's "sardonic smile"—the Russian really was only joking—but no matter: He's had enough. "The British Parliament and public will never tolerate mass executions!" he thunders. "The Soviets must be under no delusion on this point."

"Fifty thousand must be shot," Stalin insists, waving his hand casually and sticking with the joke.

"I would rather be taken out into the garden here and now and be shot myself than sully my own and my country's honor by such infamy!" Churchill roars.

Roosevelt, startled by the exchange, tries to defuse the tension. Perhaps only forty-nine thousand need be shot rather than fifty thousand, he suggests, making his best attempt at humor. His quip does not help. Churchill is tired of being ganged up on. He storms out, heading for the back garden.

Chomping on his cigar and standing in the garden, he's still fuming, but as he gazes out into the night, he feels a hand on his shoulder.

It's Stalin.

He and Molotov have come out to reassure Churchill that it was all just a joke. They want to make amends. Churchill calms down, and they walk back in together. The Prime Minister is still offended that Stalin said he was being soft on Germany. Back in the dining room, he declares to the Soviet Premier, "I'd like to go to your front, and I'm in my seventieth year!"

The evening continues for a few more hours before the participants make their way to bed. For Churchill, it's been a brutal two days. His closest ally seems to have taken against him, his integrity's been questioned . . . it's all been a mess. Thankfully, tomorrow is his birthday.

That alone should make it better.

46

The NKVD have the Nazis in their sights.

There are six in total, working out of a safehouse and using a radio transmitter to send encrypted messages back to Berlin. As the Soviets already told the Americans and the British, the Nazis are planning the "assassination or abduction of the Big Three." These six are the advance team, while the real commandos to come are "to be led by Skorzeny."

For the Soviets, this is the fork in the road. Time to make a choice.

They can continue to monitor the Germans and deliberately allow the mission to proceed. With their advance knowledge of what's to come, they can intercept, overwhelm, and capture or kill the commando team when it arrives—including its mythic leader.

"It was tempting to seize Skorzeny himself," Gevork Vartanian later admitted, knowing the accolades this would bring.

The problem is that passively awaiting the arrival of a well-armed team of Nazi commandos is an extremely dangerous thing to do. If Skorzeny's team manages to harm the Allied leaders—or even if they fail but still kill some Allied soldiers in the attempt, the responsibility will fall squarely on the shoulders of the NKVD agents who allowed them to come.

One option is to storm in now and either kill the six Germans or throw them in a Soviet prison. But in that scenario they would lose their one way to track Skorzeny and his team's arrival and whereabouts.

Instead, they come up with something slightly more nuanced. On November 28 or 29—according to Vartanian, it's during the first two days of the conference—they burst into the safehouse and arrest the six Nazi agents. Then they force one of the Germans to make a radio report to Berlin saying that they've been captured. It's a clever strategy. Once Berlin hears that the mission has been discovered, hopefully they'll call it off.

The only question is, will the Germans believe it?

47

— NOVEMBER 30, 1943 —

It's Winston Churchill's birthday, and for the third day in a row, the sun is shining in Tehran.

Overall, Roosevelt can feel his grand plan working. He's got at least some of Stalin's trust, and together they've put maximum pressure on Churchill. But at last night's dinner, he saw that Churchill had nearly reached his breaking point. Roosevelt had wanted to reach out to his friend, but he couldn't risk any nearby Soviets seeing the two of them talking in private. That would immediately get reported to Stalin and set everything back.

Instead, Roosevelt sent his close friend, Harry Hopkins,

whom Churchill is fond of, to speak candidly with the Prime Minister. There's no record of what exactly Hopkins said to Churchill, but the message, delivered in a kindly tone, was this: Churchill was "fighting a losing battle in trying to delay the invasion of France," that "there was really little Churchill could do," and that the Prime Minister should "yield with grace."

Whether or not Hopkins's visit did the trick, Churchill does—thankfully—seem to be yielding with grace. By the end of the morning of the third day of the summit, he's on board and on board completely. He'll accept a set date for the cross-Channel attack.

Immediately, the American and British military leaders get down to work, conducting smaller meetings to work through the details. Meanwhile, the President and the Prime Minister invite Stalin for lunch, where Roosevelt announces that the Combined Chiefs of Staff have forged a plan for Overlord, and that the Americans and British fully agree on it.

He reads the top line of the report for Stalin: "We will launch Overlord during May, in conjunction with a supporting operation against the south of France on the largest scale that is permitted by the landing craft available at the time." Finally, a guarantee of a cross-Channel invasion.

They'll pick a date in May without delay and promise that the Mediterranean operations will not interfere with the cross-Channel attack.

Ambassador Harriman is also at the table, and he witnesses the Soviet Premier's reaction. "Stalin, who had waited two years to hear those words, showed great satisfaction," he later recalled.

Even so, it's Churchill who seems to be the excited one. His sore throat is better, and his sour mood has lifted. It is his birthday, after all. Now that the decision had been taken, he declares to the room, "Overlord should be delivered with *smashing force*" (italics added).

Stalin thinks it likely that Hitler will try to "transfer troops from the eastern front to oppose Overlord" and promises that the Red Army will "launch simultaneously with Overlord large scale offensives in a number of places for the purpose of pinning down German forces and preventing the transfer of German troops to the west."

Now that they're all on the same page, the ideas are flowing. Stalin informs Roosevelt and Churchill that his armies often create decoy military operations to lure the Germans in the wrong direction, thereby concealing and protecting their true mission. Roosevelt and Churchill agree to create for Overlord a "cover plan . . . to confuse and deceive the enemy as to the real time and place of [the] joint blows."

Churchill declares that the "truth deserves a bodyguard of lies"!

The energy couldn't be more different from that of the previous day. Indeed, the mood is so positive, the leaders agree to end the session early. There are plenty of other topics to discuss, but they'll cover those during the final daytime meetings tomorrow.

For now, it's time to celebrate.

48

From the moment Churchill said he would host his own birthday party, his staff has been scrambling around the clock.

The menu, the silverware, the music, the drinks—everything has to be perfect. Unlike the previous dinners, this one will be held at the British embassy, a few hundred yards from the Soviet embassy across a cordoned-off street. Since the front entrance has a steep flight of stairs, the staff build a ramp to accommodate Roosevelt's wheelchair.

The security teams are also busy. The US Secret Service, led by Mike Reilly, does a full survey of the grounds and interior. They comb every shrub outside and every piece of furniture inside, searching for bombs, explosives, or any evidence of enemy activity. They find nothing. When they finish, the Soviet security team takes over and repeats the process, step by step.

Churchill is in fine form, greeting the arriving guests outside the building. Just before 8:30 p.m., Roosevelt arrives, and the two men greet each other warmly. For three days, Roosevelt has been cagey with Churchill, keeping him at arm's length in order to establish rapport with Stalin. Now, the need for gamesmanship is gone.

Stalin's entrance, a few minutes later, does not go as smoothly. After he and Molotov climb the front steps, a young member of the British staff innocently approaches to help the Soviet Premier remove his cape. In an instant, NKVD agents close in. One of them grabs the young man, another sticks a pistol in his ribs, and they roughly drag him off down the hall.

After the scuffle is over and calm is restored, the guests make their way to the dining room. Greetings are exchanged, and seats taken. The three Allied leaders sit side by side at the head of the table, with the birthday host between the other two.

Churchill has decided that instead of making speeches,

they'll follow the Russian tradition of giving plentiful toasts. So, as the guests start eating, the toasts start flowing, as do the accompanying glasses of vodka, whiskey, and wine. Roosevelt starts with a ceremonial toast to King George VI of the United Kingdom. Churchill follows with a toast to the President of the United States of America. Roosevelt, he says with feeling, is "a man who [has] devoted his entire life to the cause of defending the weak and helpless, and to the promotion of the great principles that underlie our democratic civilization."

Next, Churchill toasts Stalin for his leadership of the Soviet armies. In the Russian tradition, he should be known as "Stalin the Great," Churchill says, getting a few laughs. Stalin raises his glass in response. But, he says of Churchill's compliments, "the honors which [have] been paid to him really [belong] to the Russian people."

Then Roosevelt raises his glass again, to say happy birthday to Churchill and to express "his joy in the friendship which [has] developed between them in the midst of their common efforts in this war." Each toast gets a warm round of applause.

Once the plates are cleared, a waiter places a massive cake in front of Churchill, containing sixty-nine candles shaped in a V for victory. It takes a few attempts, but

Churchill eventually manages to blow them all out.

As the party goes on, there's one person who's clearly not enjoying himself.

Mike Reilly.

All evening, he stands along the wall, eyes darting, trying to study every part of the room at once. For three days, he has been on edge, constantly worried about the President's safety. His experience at the conference began with the news of Nazi parachutists and hidden assassins, and he hasn't been able to relax since.

As the dinner ends and everyone's about to get up from the table, Roosevelt asks if he may give one more toast. Raising his glass, he toasts the people of the United States, the United Kingdom, and the Soviet Union. Looking around the room, he says,

> *We have differing customs and philosophies and ways of life. Each of us works out our scheme of things according to the desires and ideas of our own peoples.*
>
> *But we have proved here at Tehran that the varying ideals of our nations can come together in a harmonious whole, moving unitedly for the common good of ourselves and of the world.*

His words get the biggest applause of the night.

At a certain point, the music is turned up, and Churchill begins to show off some dance moves. Before anyone can stop him, he kicks up his short legs in a traditional Scottish hornpipe.

Mike Reilly is too nervous to enjoy the spectacle.

If he could see just a little into the future, he'd know that the evening will end just fine. By 2 a.m. or so, all the guests will be safely back in their quarters. Whatever potential assassins are out there never make it to the party. And within thirty-six hours, the three Allied leaders will all be gone from the city without incident.

Reilly doesn't know this yet, so he can't possibly be at ease. But there's someone in the room who is: Franklin Roosevelt. This conference was his vision more than anyone else's. For more than a year, he fought for it, overcoming every imaginable obstacle. Many times, it seemed like it would never take place. But it did. Here, in the city of Tehran, the three Allied leaders came together, and in a few days' time, the photographs will be seen around the world, creating a surge of confidence on the Allied side.

The road ahead is long, and there are many dark and difficult days to come. But tonight, in this room, there are some moments to savor.

His grand vision for a Big Three summit has been realized.

The three leaders set aside their differences and forged a plan to end this terrible war and destroy the tyrannical Nazi regime that started it.

The Allied leaders have avoided an assassination plot.

And Winston Churchill is dancing.

The spirit of cooperation Roosevelt experiences at the conference fills him with enormous optimism—not just for the Allied war effort but also for the world peace that will follow victory. Just before leaving Tehran, the three leaders sign a "Declaration of the Three Powers," now known as the Tehran Declaration, which they share with the press a few days later.

The declaration begins, "We, the President of the United States, the Prime Minister of Great Britain, and the Premier of the Soviet Union, have met these four days past, in this, the capital of our ally, Iran, and have shaped and confirmed our common policy." It goes on to promise that the Allies will "win an enduring peace . . . which will command the good will of the overwhelming mass of the peoples of the world and banish the scourge and terror of war for many generations."

As well as these noble sentiments, the declaration

asserts that plans have been made for "the destruction of the German forces" and that "we have reached complete agreement as to the scope and timing of the operations to be undertaken from the east, west, and south. The common understanding which we have here reached guarantees that victory will be ours."

It's the promise of victory that dominates the news. While the leaders' declaration provides no military specifics, the press starts digging and soon reports that Roosevelt, Churchill, and Stalin agreed in Tehran to the operation the Allied world has long awaited: an Anglo-American attack against Nazi forces in Western Europe, to take place in the spring of 1944.

Now comes the hard part. They have to deliver.

49

— SPRING 1944 —

For two years they've discussed it, debated it, dissected it, revised it, renamed it, and—repeatedly—postponed it.

Operation Overlord. The cross-Channel attack.

By the time Roosevelt returns to the United States, in late December 1943, planning is in high gear. Overlord's supreme commander, US General Dwight D. Eisenhower, considers several places for an amphibious landing before settling on a long stretch of beaches in the Normandy region of northern France.

Military planners divide the roughly fifty-mile stretch

into five adjacent zones, code-named Utah, Omaha, Gold, Juno, and Sword. What follows will be the largest combined operation in the history of warfare. The first wave alone will involve 5,300 ships, 1,500 tanks, 12,000 aircraft, and 150,000 soldiers, with a total of 1 million troops at the ready to join the mission in the following weeks.

Just as the three Allied leaders discussed in Tehran, deception will have an important part to play in the operation's success. The planners craft a complex series of decoy missions, complete with elaborate command structures, aircraft and naval movements, ghost armies, and radio traffic. The organization of these dummy missions is such a huge undertaking that it gets its own name, Operation Bodyguard, named after the phrase Churchill used in Tehran, "a bodyguard of lies."

The Nazis know the Americans and British are coming. They know that they'll attack Western Europe sometime in spring, probably in France. What they don't know is exactly where or when. Because of poor weather and other factors, the operation is delayed for several weeks past the May deadline. Then, in the early hours of June 6, 1944, German soldiers in northern France spot Allied paratroopers in the skies.

The first landing craft approach the shore in the early

light. On Utah, the westernmost beach, US troops meet only minor resistance. Likewise, on Gold, Juno, and Sword, assorted British and Canadian troops make their landings with moderate casualties. But on Omaha, everything goes wrong. The storm-swept sea is much rougher than expected. The landing craft encounter sandbars and can't get close enough to shore. Enemy artillery starts to rain down on the boats, creating chaos, and panicking soldiers tumble from the landing craft only to drown in the freezing waters. Several tanks slide off the landing craft and sink in the Channel, taking their crews with them.

The soldiers who don't drown find themselves neck-deep in frigid water. Carrying twenty pounds of gear, they slowly push toward shore, their rifles held above their heads. As the first wave of soldiers stumble onto the beach, they're instantly cut down by German machine guns and artillery firing at them from the bluffs above the shoreline and from the sand dunes.

In several hours of fighting, eight hundred US soldiers die, and casualties continue to mount throughout the long day and night. After twenty-four hours, the total number of US, British, and Canadian casualties is roughly ten thousand, with a similar number on the German side.

But the ships and the soldiers keep coming. By midday,

they've established a footing, and by afternoon some of them have reached the bluffs of the beach. By midnight of the next day, June 7, over one hundred fifty thousand troops have landed on the Normandy coast.

Strategically, the consequences of the landing are enormous. The Allies now have a protected entry point into Western Europe. By the end of June, after three weeks of fierce combat, they have a secure foothold in northwestern France. From here, they can start to move across the French countryside, slowly but steadily, in the direction of Berlin.

Hitler and his commanders would like to throw the entire might of the German army at the approaching American and British ground forces. But they can't. Thousands of miles away, the massive Soviet armies along the Eastern Front are also on the move, pushing relentlessly toward Germany from the other side.

There are many dark days and terrible battles ahead.

But the end is in sight.

50

— SUMMER 1944 —

When the Allies began their advance through France toward Berlin, some military leaders thought that the war in Europe would end quickly.

With the largest and most powerful military units in the world closing in on either side, Germany's position was clearly hopeless. The Wehrmacht was battered, its forces depleted. Hitler's refusal to surrender at this point was one of the many incalculable tragedies of the war. Armies on both sides had to keep fighting, battle after battle, with senseless casualties mounting for everyone involved.

The suffering of innocent populations never ceased—if anything, the toll inflicted on civilians grew worse. Before invading Normandy, the Allies carried out bombing raids in France to destroy bridges, roads, factories, and other targets that might be useful to the occupying German troops. These raids were successful, but they caused over forty thousand civilian deaths. And as Soviet troops surged westward through Eastern Europe, they exacted brutal revenge on local populations and groups they suspected of collaboration with the Germans.

On the night of July 22, Red Army soldiers approach what appears to be a series of barracks in Lublin, Poland. They've entered the Majdanek death camp, vacated by the SS only a few days before.

They are horrified by what they find. The camp is mostly empty now, but the evidence of atrocities is clear, including the zigzagging trenches where, eight months earlier, SS guards massacred and buried eighteen thousand Jewish prisoners during Operation Harvest Festival. Majdanek is the first Nazi death camp to be discovered and liberated by Allied forces. Many more are soon to come. As researchers, journalists, and forensic experts begin to study the evidence, the overwhelming scope and horror of the Nazi death program becomes sickeningly clear.

51

Berlin, Germany

— APRIL 30, 1945 —

A pistol and a cyanide pill.

The Führer, Adolf Hitler, carries these with him to the *Führerbunker,* his underground study beneath the Reich Chancellery Garden in Berlin. Much of the city above him is in ruins from American bombs and Soviet artillery. Five months earlier, in November 1944, he fled the Wolf's Lair when the Red Army reached East Prussia.

He now sits on a small couch in the study. At roughly 3:15 p.m., he raises the pistol to his right temple and pulls the trigger.

The Führer is dead.

He was, in Churchill's words, "the repository and expression of the most virulent hatreds that have ever corroded the human breast."

However, it wasn't just Hitler. It was an entire regime. A hateful ideology that began decades earlier was allowed to fester and to grow. First, it gripped a political party, then it spread to an entire nation. Every one of Hitler's appalling decisions was supported by countless enablers and collaborators within a vast, powerful political and cultural movement.

But now, the Nazi Party is finished. In the coming days and weeks, American and Soviet forces will take over Berlin, and the Allies will scour Germany and the former Axis territories to find and arrest any Nazi officials who are not already captured or dead.

Among those apprehended was Walter Schellenberg, the former foreign intelligence leader. The British find him in Denmark in June 1945.

For several months before the end of the war, along with SS leader Heinrich Himmler, Schellenberg had been secretly trying to negotiate peace terms with the Allies behind Hitler's back. Schellenberg convinced Himmler that there was a chance they could salvage some elements of the German government and stop the Allies from destroying Berlin. But, as Roosevelt had promised at the Casablanca conference back in early 1943, the Allies required *unconditional surrender.* They were never going to negotiate with Himmler or Schellenberg, or any other Nazi leader.

Upon hearing about Schellenberg's position as head of foreign intelligence, the British requested that he be transferred to London for extensive interrogation. After his arrest, Schellenberg tried to position himself as a friend to the Allies. He had no part in planning the war, he told them, and he was not personally responsible for any atrocities committed by the Nazi leadership.

In the end, they charged him with a few relatively modest crimes, and he later testified at the Nuremberg trials, where Nazi leaders were charged with war crimes and crimes against humanity. Schellenberg was forthcoming with information that implicated others but careful not to incriminate himself.

Unlike many of his former colleagues of similar or higher rank, Schellenberg was spared the death penalty. Instead, the Court sentenced him to six years in prison. After two years, he was released due to ill health. He died in 1952, at the age of forty-two.

Another Nazi caught in the Allies' dragnet was Otto

Skorzeny, the infamous rescuer of Benito Mussolini. Skorzeny had become one of Hitler's favorite military officers and had received increasingly prestigious military commands. He had led German forces in Western Europe, as well as in battles against the Soviets during the Red Army's final push through Eastern Europe to Berlin.

On May 16, 1945, a week after the end of the war was declared, Skorzeny turned himself in to the Americans. At first, they treated him like any other captured enemy officer, but when they realized who he really was, Skorzeny later described, "a dozen submachine-guns were pointing at me and the interpreter asked me to hand over my pistol, which I did . . . Then I was frisked and stripped naked."

For the next two years, US and British officials transferred Skorzeny from city to city and from prison to prison. The intelligence services interrogated him dozens of times. He occasionally endured rough treatment, including solitary confinement and sleep deprivation.

His most famous act—the rescue of Mussolini—was not a war crime, but Skorzeny faced charges for other activities, including the alleged murder of Allied POWs. Ultimately, he was acquitted by the Nuremberg tribunal, but he still faced lengthy detention as part of the Allied "denazification" program. In 1948, he escaped from Allied detention in a complex plot involving three Germans dressed as US officers. Since he had never been charged with a crime, international authorities didn't waste any resources tracking him down.

Despite all the interrogations both Skorzeny and Schellenberg endured in Allied custody, neither ever said a word—nor apparently was ever asked—about the alleged plot to kill Roosevelt, Stalin, and Churchill at the Tehran Conference in November 1943.

The entire episode seems to have been forgotten.

But that doesn't mean it has completely gone away.

52

In the months and years following the Big Three conference in Tehran, not much was publicly said or written about the assassination plot. Behind the scenes, however, some of the details were questioned—as was the plot itself.

Joe Spencer, the head of the British intelligence office in Tehran, claimed that the story of the plot was unreliable, simply because he himself had not seen any evidence of it. He believed that his team had successfully cleared the city of most, if not all, German agents.

Spencer oversaw British intelligence in the region

before and during the conference, so his opinion shouldn't be ignored. But it's also true that he didn't know everything about Nazi activities in Iran. In fact, he couldn't have.

The Soviets and the British may have been allies during the war, but the relationship was one characterized by rivalry and distrust. At the time, security and intelligence in Iran were divided between the British and the Soviets, with the British in charge of the southern half of the country and the Soviets in charge of the north. Tehran was a shared effort. Because every report of the assassination plot came from the Soviet side, it's possible—and even likely—that British intelligence wouldn't have known about the German agents the Soviets were tracking.

Spencer's comments also reflect his own self-interest. As the person charged with knowing about enemy activity in Iran, he might have been embarrassed to learn that the Soviets discovered thirty-eight Nazi paratroopers and a plot so dangerous it caused the Americans to move their President across the city huddled in the back of a beat-up car. His dismissal of the plot might simply be a way to save face and protect the reputation of his agency.

But Spencer wasn't the only one to throw cold water on the idea of an assassination plot. Averell Harriman,

Roosevelt's Ambassador to the Soviet Union, who first reported the plot to the President based on the account he heard from Vyacheslav Molotov, left the conference with some nagging doubts about what had transpired.

Soon after the summit, Harriman found himself in a room with Molotov and decided to ask the Foreign Minister how serious the plot really was. "He said they had taken precautions because of rumors. He never said there was a specific plot," Harriman later reported. The conversation left Harriman unsure as to whether a Nazi plot ever really existed.

Harriman's skepticism was counterbalanced by others who attended the conference and who believed that the plot was most definitely real. Churchill himself asserted afterward that he was sure there had been a plot to kill the Big Three, and his certainty was matched by his personal head of security during the conference, police detective Walter H. "Tommy" Thompson. Thompson claimed that he had learned, presumably through conversations with NKVD agents, of at least sixty German parachutists who had landed in or near Tehran on the eve of the conference and that many of those captured were armed with guns and explosives.

Of all the Americans who were in Tehran at the time of

the conference, it was Mike Reilly, Roosevelt's head of security, who heard the most comprehensive version of the plot from Soviet sources. Reilly's job was to determine credible threats to the President and to separate them from rumors and hoaxes. He had a lot of experience at this, during both peacetime and war, and he found the NKVD reports to be entirely legitimate. It's why he persuaded Roosevelt to get into a decoy car and move to the Soviet embassy while a fake motorcade distracted any unwelcome attention. Reilly never doubted the veracity of the NKVD's claims about the plot, even years later when he wrote his memoir.

In the years following the end of the war, the murkiness of the assassination plot was made even murkier by the fact that the only people who knew for certain the extent and detail of the plot—namely, the Nazis who planned it—would never, ever admit to it.

After the war, thirty-seven Nazi officials were convicted of war crimes and sentenced to death. Many more received long prison terms. If any Nazi official or German military officer revealed their participation in—or knowledge of—a plot to kill the Allied leaders, they would be in serious trouble. For this reason, the lack of witnesses or of any paper trail on the German side is unsurprising. All evidence would have been destroyed.

With that said, it's impossible to ignore one simple detail. If there wasn't a real Nazi assassination plot against the Big Three, then why would the Soviets invent one? Why would they notify the Americans, at midnight on the night before the conference began, that the President's life was in danger and urge them to move Roosevelt and his entire delegation across the city?

The answer to these questions adds another wrinkle to the story.

In November 1943, young Sergo Beria traveled to the conference in Tehran with his father, Lavrentiy Beria—the notorious head of the NKVD. Because Sergo knew how to speak and read English, Stalin gave him a special assignment. Every morning, he was to translate from English to Russian some recordings that had been made the night before.

The source of these recordings? Audio obtained from secret microphones hidden within the American villa at the Soviet embassy.

The young man followed orders, and every morning at 6 o'clock, he listened to, translated, and transcribed the recordings of President Franklin D. Roosevelt talking with his aides. At precisely 8 a.m., he shared the transcripts with Stalin.

Beria's account has not been proven and is probably not provable. But it is plausible. Stalin was famous for secretly recording enemies and allies alike. The possibility that he bugged Roosevelt's villa supports the theory that the Soviets made up the Nazi plot so they could get Roosevelt into a place where they could eavesdrop on him.

Some have argued that if Beria's account is true, Roosevelt was gullible to allow his private conversations to be heard by a foreign leader at an event of such critical importance. But it's also possible, as others have suggested, that Roosevelt and his team were experienced enough with Stalin that they would have *assumed* any room within the Soviet embassy was bugged anyway. In that case, Roosevelt would have intentionally only said things he wanted Stalin to hear.

In other words, he would be using the fact that his room was bugged as a tool to manipulate the Soviets. If that is true, it means a whole other layer of gamesmanship was going on during the Tehran summit beyond what transpired in the conference rooms.

As time passed, the story of the assassination plot became colored by the Cold War, an era of rising hostility between the West and the Soviet Union. Under the rhetoric of those times, the Americans and the British couldn't allow the Soviets to be the heroes who had saved the day. Instead, it had to be that the plot was all a hoax to deceive and manipulate Roosevelt.

Meanwhile, the Soviet framing of the story was that Soviet intelligence services had thwarted a Nazi plot that could have killed the Allied leaders. For this, the Western world should owe them a debt of gratitude.

These diverging views reflected increasing tensions between the Soviet Union and the West about how the war was remembered. The Soviets resented the United States and the UK for downplaying, or simply forgetting, the role of the Soviets in defeating Nazi Germany. To prove their point, they could point to many Western portrayals of the war—Hollywood movies, newsreels, radio programs, and even history schoolbooks—in which the United States and Great Britain heroically saved the world from Hitler while the USSR was barely mentioned, if at all.

These grievances came from a deep place.

During World War II, it was the Soviets who did most of the fighting and dying against the Nazis. The United States suffered an estimated 419,000 war-related deaths and the UK an estimated 451,000—large numbers to be sure. But the Soviet Union lost at least 24 million lives to the war: over twenty-five times more than the United

States and UK combined. In terms of sheer sacrifice, there's simply no comparison.

One thing we do know is that in the fall of 1943, the Germans were desperate to turn the tide of the war. That year, the Nazi armies experienced a series of brutal defeats on the battlefield. The Wehrmacht remained a mighty force, but it was growing steadily weaker as the Allied forces grew stronger. Germany's only real "victory" during this period was Skorzeny's rescue of Mussolini, but this rescue, however remarkable, could hardly influence the military course of the war.

It's not hard to imagine that the Nazi leadership would seize the opportunity to strike against the Big Three. The cost of failure would be minimal—the loss of a few dozen men, perhaps—but the rewards if they succeeded would be immense. Assassinating Roosevelt, Stalin, and Churchill—or even just one of them—would have been so earth-shattering, and such a huge blow to the Allies, that the war effort would have changed overnight in ways almost impossible to fathom.

Furthermore, once the Nazis learned of the summit's probable location of Tehran, the idea of launching a clandestine assassination mission would have been almost irresistible. They already had an infrastructure in place for parachuting armed commando teams into Iran and a network of agents and sympathizers on the ground ready to support any such operation.

It may well be that the Soviets bugged Roosevelt's quarters during his stay at the Soviet embassy in Tehran. If so, does it prove that they made up the assassination plot to lure him into an eavesdropping trap?

The answer is no. Because, quite simply, two things can be true at the same time.

On the one hand, the NKVD could have been genuinely worried about a Nazi plot to kill the Big Three and believed that Roosevelt should move to the Soviet embassy to avoid the three leaders crossing the city. At the same time, once the decision was made for Roosevelt to move to the Soviet embassy, Stalin could have realized that there was an opportunity to eavesdrop on him.

One truth does not cancel the other. In fact, both make sense based on everything known about the Soviets and their preparations for the summit.

On the German side, the lack of a paper trail doesn't prove or disprove much of anything. After the war, the SD destroyed every sensitive document in their possession.

What is known for sure is that the Nazis were willing and able to use assassination as a tool of war. Schellenberg himself wrote about a 1944 plot to assassinate Stalin in Moscow. A high-level Nazi, possibly Heinrich Himmler, would enter the Kremlin on a diplomatic mission, and then, as soon as he was in a room with Stalin, he would pull out a concealed pistol and shoot the Soviet Premier before he himself was shot by the guards. The very existence of this plot, apparently conceived by Hitler himself, removes any doubt that the Nazis would have hesitated to kill the Allied leaders.

In the 1960s, a renewed public appetite for World War II espionage stories led to several sensationalized and semi-fictionalized treatments of the plot. It was during this period that Otto Skorzeny, famed rescuer of Mussolini, came forward to respond to journalists who'd reached out to him about the story. His name had been mentioned repeatedly in conjunction with the plot, and he wanted to set the record straight. He would also address rumors of the plot in some of his memoirs.

Skorzeny blamed his old boss for the whole business. "I believe that Walter Schellenberg was enthusiastic about the idea of planning an action against the 'big three' enemies of Germany," he asserted. In seeking to distance himself from the plot, Skorzeny revealed a remarkable detail: He and Schellenberg met with Hitler at the Wolf's Lair in early

November 1943, specifically to talk about the possibility of assassinating the Big Three in Tehran. Skorzeny claimed that he wanted nothing to do with such an operation. He said that at the time he reviewed the available intelligence on Tehran and decided "the plan was simply impractical," declining to participate.

It's hard to see why Skorzeny would make up the story of the meeting, especially so long after the fact. But his denial of any involvement in the plot is inconclusive. Former Nazi war criminals were not immune from prosecution, and the last thing Skorzeny would have wanted was a new charge against him. His denial, then, could have been his way of taking any remaining suspicion off himself and instead putting it on someone who was already dead.

Also, he never did like Walter Schellenberg.

Some aspects of the story will probably always be uncertain. New evidence might come to light if researchers are ever allowed access to the archives of the Russian Foreign Intelligence Service. But even then, some details will probably remain unclear.

However, while researchers and historians continue to debate the details, there's one conclusion upon which even the most skeptical and the most sensational accounts of the plot usually agree. Its ultimate failure rests in large part on the shoulders of one man.

Paradoxically, he's someone who didn't even know about the assassination plot's existence.

Franz Mayr.

The minute the British arrested Mayr, Nazi capabilities in Tehran were severely crippled, and any assassination mission was probably doomed. Nazi foreign intelligence didn't know this until much later because they were unaware of Mayr's arrest for a long time. Their belief that their man on the ground in Tehran was operational might have been what led them to think the mission was even possible.

This raises the question: Whatever became of Franz Mayr?

After his arrest, Mayr spent a lot of time in a very uncomfortable place: the interrogation room. According to his British captors, at first, he "resisted interrogation with considerable energy," but soon he succumbed to the pressure and offered up all he knew, including the whereabouts of the remaining members of Operation Franz.

In late 1943, the British transferred Mayr from Tehran to Cairo. After the war, he remained in Allied custody, but in 1946 he escaped and made his way to Switzerland. The Swiss authorities arrested him for illegal entry and sent him to occupied Germany, which was then controlled by the Allies, where he promptly escaped again. From there, Mayr began a long period of moving from place to place, with years spent in Austria, Switzerland, Italy, Spain, Portugal, Lebanon, Egypt, and Syria.

He found success managing an import–export firm based in Hamburg, Germany, but his business may have also been a front for political activities, including the recruitment of former SS officers to work for Middle Eastern governments. Little is known of his life beyond that point, and it's not clear when or where he died.

Shortly after his arrest, Mayr asked the British authorities, just as he had once asked his German superiors, for permission to marry his girlfriend, Lili Sanjari. It's not clear how he expected his British captors to honor this extraordinary request. In any case, they refused, and Mayr likely never saw Sanjari again.

About her, nothing more is known. After Mayr was arrested, the British authorities simply lost interest in her. The Germans came and went, and the Allies came and went, but for all we know, Lili Sanjari stayed in Tehran.

53

The President never gets to see the end.

Back in the United States, FDR wins reelection as President in a landslide—432 electoral votes to 99—but the long Presidential campaign has exhausted him and taken a toll on his health. Everyone can see that he looks paler, more gaunt, with bags under his eyes.

On a frigid Inauguration Day, January 20, 1945, he's sworn in for a fourth term.

Instead of the usual parade, he gives a speech on the South Portico of the White House. "We have learned that we cannot live alone, at peace; that our own well-being is dependent on the well-being of other nations far away," he declares. "We have learned to be citizens of the world . . . We have learned . . . 'The only way to have a friend is to be one.'"

What drives Roosevelt now is his vision for the peace that is coming. After fighting this long and terrible war, and with victory over fascism so near, he desperately wants to implement his ideals for lasting postwar harmony. It's this desire that brings the Big Three together one last time.

As before, it's Roosevelt who urges for a conference, this time for early 1945. Despite the American President's poor health, Stalin again insists that the other leaders travel across the world to meet him. Ironically, he cites his own health as the reason why he can't travel far. Roosevelt agrees to the condition and urges Churchill to do the same. A face-to-face conference is too important to miss.

A long journey takes Roosevelt by ship to the island of Malta in the Mediterranean for preliminary discussions with Churchill. Then, together, they fly to Yalta, a resort town on the Black Sea, where Stalin is waiting for them. On February 4, the three leaders meet again. This time, they don't call it a war conference—it is a peace conference.

Roosevelt looks pale for much of the Yalta conference, wearing a heavy shawl around his shoulders as his aides push him from place to place. On his return to the United States, he goes to his favorite place in the world: Warm Springs, Georgia, where, decades before, he went to recover from polio. He is planning a long stay to recover his energy and his health.

By this point, Allied troops are in Germany, approaching Berlin from multiple directions. The circle is getting smaller; victory is so close.

But Hitler won't stop fighting. Rather than surrender Berlin, he orders the Hitler Youth—boys and teenagers—to join what's left of the battered German armies defending the city. It's a hopeless cause, and when Allied tanks and troops storm the burning capital, thousands of German youths, some as young as twelve, die in the carnage.

On April 12, Roosevelt begins the day in Warm Springs, hoping for rest and recovery. Although the weather is fine, he feels a chill and asks for a cape to put over his shoulders. He complains of a headache and a stiff neck, which seem to get better after a massage.

Later that morning, he sits for a portrait. The artist, Elizabeth Shoumatoff, notices that he has some color back in his face. Roosevelt is seated in a chair at a card table that serves as a makeshift desk, reading the newspaper and writing some letters while Shoumatoff paints. Suddenly, his head droops forward, and he puts a hand on the back of his neck. "I have a terrific pain in the back of my head," he says, and slumps to the floor. He loses consciousness, and never regains it.

At 3:35 p.m., the doctor pronounces President Franklin Delano Roosevelt dead.

Within minutes of the announcement, the news reaches London. "I felt as if I had been struck by a physical blow," Winston Churchill later recalled. For months, he's been dreaming of the day when he and Roosevelt, together, would celebrate victory in Europe. Instead, he is "overwhelmed by a sense of deep and irrefutable loss."

It isn't just the heads of state who are devastated.

That same morning, back in Georgia, the President's family is making last-minute arrangements for his body to travel to Washington, DC.

The Warm Springs Rehabilitation facility has a long-standing tradition that at the end of one of Roosevelt's many visits, the other camp attendees, many of them children afflicted with polio, would gather outside the main hall near the camp's entrance to say goodbye to him in person. Today, they gather again, this time to say goodbye for good. Sitting in wheelchairs and leaning on arm braces, they watch as an open hearse carrying a flag-draped coffin slowly drives past.

"The child patients were sobbing," the President's secretary, Grace Tully, later recalled. "The adults sobbed too."

A few soldiers and musicians from nearby Fort Benning have been sent to join the small makeshift procession. As the hearse passes by, one of Roosevelt's favorite musicians, a Chief Petty Officer named Graham W. Jackson, steps forward with an accordion and plays a piece called "Going Home." He, too, has tears streaming down his face.

Several hours later, the Presidential train arrives in Washington, DC, bearing the coffin. Here, another procession is waiting, but this one isn't small. It's a crowd of half a million people, gathered at the National Mall, many of whom have traveled from all over the country to pay tribute.

He led the nation through the darkest days of war. Now peace is coming, and the President, Franklin Delano Roosevelt, is finally, truly, at rest.

SELECTED BIBLIOGRAPHY

Bates, John L. "The 'Eureka' Conference: A Busy Time in Teheran." *Military Review* 66, no. 10 (October 1986): 74–82.

Bazna, Elyesa. *I Was Cicero*. Translated by Eric Mosbacher. New York: Harper & Row, 1962.

Beevor, Antony. *The Second World War*. New York: Little, Brown, 2012.

Bell, Leland V. "The Failure of Nazism in America: The German American Bund, 1936–1941." *Political Science Quarterly* 85, no. 4 (December 1970): 585–99.

Beorn, Waitman Wade. *The Holocaust in Eastern Europe: At the Epicenter of the Final Solution*. London: Bloomsbury, 2018.

Beria, Sergo. *Beria, My Father: Inside Stalin's Kremlin*. Edited by Françoise Thom. Translated by Brian Pearce. London: Duckworth, 2001.

Blandford, Edmund L. *SS Intelligence: The Nazi Secret Service.* Edison, NJ: Castle Books, 2001.

Blum, Howard. *Night of the Assassins: The Untold Story of Hitler's Plot to Kill FDR, Churchill, and Stalin.* New York: HarperCollins, 2020.

Bohlen, Charles E. *Witness to History, 1929–1969.* New York: W. W. Norton, 1973.

Breitman, Richard, and Allan J. Lichtman. *FDR and the Jews.* Cambridge, MA: Harvard University Press, 2013.

"Broadcast by Churchill from Quebec: 'Drive On Until We Have Finished the Job,'" *Morning Bulletin* (Rockhampton), September 2, 1943, pp. 1, 4. https://trove.nla.gov.au/newspaper/article/56288916/5448880.

Butler, Susan, ed. *My Dear Mr. Stalin: The Complete Correspondence of Franklin D. Roosevelt and Joseph V. Stalin.* New Haven, CT: Yale University Press, 2006.

Churchill, Winston. "Blood, Toil, Tears and Sweat: First Speech as Prime Minister to the House of Commons, May 13, 1940." International Churchill Society. https://winstonchurchill.org/resources/speeches/1940-the-finest-hour/blood-toil-tears-sweat.

———. Broadcast on the Soviet–German War, June 22, 1941. www.jewishvirtuallibrary.org/churchill-broadcast-on-the-soviet-german-war-june-1941.

———. *The Second World War.* 6 vols. Boston: Houghton Mifflin, 1948–1953.

Clark, Lloyd. "The Largest Tank Battle in History Began 75 Years Ago Today—Here's How It Changed WWII." *Military Times*, July 5, 2018. www.militarytimes.com/veterans/military-history/2018/07/05/the-largest-tank-battle-in-history-began-75-years-ago-today-heres-how-it-changed-wwii.

Doerries, Reinhard R. *Hitler's Intelligence Chief: Walter Schellenberg.* New York: Enigma Books, 2009.

———. *Hitler's Last Chief of Foreign Intelligence: Allied Interrogations of Walter Schellenberg.* London: Frank Cass, 2003.

Dolgopolov, Nikolai. "How 'the Lion and the Bear' Were Saved." *Russia Beyond the Headlines*, November 29, 2007. www.rbth.com/articles/2007/11/29/lion_and_bear.html.

———. "Triple Jeopardy: The Nazi Plan to Kill WWII Leaders in Tehran." *Sputnik International*, January 4, 2007. http://sputniknews.com/20070104/94756632.html.

———. *Vartanian: zhizn' zamechatel'nykh liudei.* Moscow: Molodaia gvardiia, 2014.

Dunn, Susan. *1940: FDR, Willkie, Lindbergh, Hitler—the Election amid the Storm.* New Haven, CT: Yale University Press, 2013.

Eubank, Keith. *Summit at Teheran: The Untold Story.* New York: William Morrow, 1985.

Evans, Richard J. *The Third Reich at War.* New York: Penguin Books, 2009.

Farago, Ladislas. *The Game of Foxes: The Untold Story of German Espionage in the United States and Great Britain during World War II*. New York: Bantam Books, 1973.

Foreign Relations of the United States: Diplomatic Papers: The Conferences at Cairo and Tehran, 1943. Washington, DC: United States Government Printing Office, 1961.

Frieser, Karl-Heinz. *Die Ostfront 1943/44: Der Krieg im Osten und an den Nebenfronten*. Munich: Deutsche Verlags-Anstalt, 2007.

Gerwarth, Robert. *Hitler's Hangman: The Life of Heydrich*. New Haven, CT: Yale University Press, 2011.

Gilbert, Martin. *Churchill: A Life*. London: Pimlico, 1991.

Goodwin, Doris Kearns. *No Ordinary Time: Franklin and Eleanor Roosevelt: The Home Front in World War II*. New York: Simon & Schuster, 1994.

Hamilton, Nigel. *Commander in Chief: FDR's Battle with Churchill, 1943*. Boston: Houghton Mifflin Harcourt, 2016.

———. *The Mantle of Command: FDR at War, 1941–1942*. Boston: Houghton Mifflin Harcourt, 2014.

———. *War and Peace: FDR's Final Odyssey D-Day to Yalta, 1943–1945*. Boston: Houghton Mifflin Harcourt, 2019.

Harriman, W. Averell, and Elie Abel. *Special Envoy to Churchill and Stalin, 1941–1946*. New York: Random House, 1975.

Harrison, Gordon A. *European Theater of Operations: Cross-Channel Attack*. Washington, DC: Department of the Army, Center for Military History, 1993.

Hastings, Max. *Inferno: The World at War, 1939–1945*. New York: Alfred A. Knopf, 2011.

Havas, Laslo. *Hitler's Plot to Kill the Big Three*. New York: Cowles Book Company, 1967.

———. *The Long Jump: The 1943 Plot to Assassinate the Big Three*. Translated by Kathleen Szasz, London: Neville Spearman, 1967.

Hett, Benjamin Carter. *The Death of Democracy: Hitler's Rise to Power and the Downfall of the Weimar Republic*. New York: Henry Holt, 2018.

Hitler, Adolf. "Adolf Hitler: Speech Declaring War against the United States (December 11, 1941)." Jewish Virtual Library. www.jewishvirtuallibrary.org/hitler-s-speech-declaring-war-against-the-united-states.

Höhne, Heinz. *Canaris: Patriot im Zwielicht*. Munich: C. Bertelsmann Verlag, 1976.

Horvitz, Leslie Alan, and Christopher Catherwood. *Encyclopedia of War Crimes and Genocide*. New York: Facts on File, 2006.

Jackson, Ashley. *Persian Gulf Command: A History of the Second World War in Iran and Iraq*. New Haven, CT: Yale University Press, 2018.

Jeffery, Inez Cope. *Inside Russia: The Life and Times of Zoya Zarubina: Former Soviet Intelligence Officer and Interpreter During the Stalin Years*, Austin, TX: Eakin Press, 1999.

Jörgensen, Christer. *Hitler's Espionage Machine: German Intelligence Agencies and Operations during World War II*. Staplehurst, UK: Spellmount, 2004.

Kahn, David. *Hitler's Spies: German Military Intelligence in World War II*. New York: Macmillan, 1978.

Katamidze, Slava. *Loyal Comrades, Ruthless Killers: The Secret Services of the USSR 1920's to the Present*, New York: Lewis International, 2003.

Kern, Gary. "How 'Uncle Joe' Bugged FDR," *Studies in Intelligence* 47, no. 1 (March 2003).

Kershaw, Ian. *Hitler, 1936–1945: Nemesis*. London: W. W. Norton, 2000.

———. *To Hell and Back: Europe 1914–1949*. New York: Penguin, 2015.

Kimball, Warren F. "A Different Take on FDR at Teheran: Raising Questions." *Studies in Intelligence* 49, no. 3 (2005).

———. *Forged in War: Roosevelt, Churchill, and the Second World War*. New York: William Morrow, 1997.

Krivosheev, G. F., ed. *Soviet Casualties and Combat Losses in the Twentieth Century*. Translated by Christine Barnard. Philadelphia: Stackpole Books, 1997.

Kuznets, Iurii. *Tehran-43*. Moscow: Eskimo, 2003.

Lord, Walter. *Day of Infamy: The Bombing of Pearl Harbor*. New York: Open Road Media, 2012.

MacDonald, Callum. *The Killing of Reinhard Heydrich: The SS "Butcher of Prague."* New York: Da Capo Press, 1989.

MacLean, Elizabeth Kimball. *Joseph E. Davies: Envoy to the Soviets.* Westport, CT: Praeger, 1992.

Mader, Julius. *Hitlers Spionagegenerale sagen aus.* Berlin: Verlag der Nation, 1970.

Medvedev, Dmitry N. *Silnyie dukhom (Eto bylo pod Rovno),* Moscow: Pravda Publishing, 1951.

Ministry of Foreign Affairs of the USSR. *Correspondence Between the Chairman of the Council of Ministers of the USSR and the Presidents of the USA and the Prime Ministers of Great Britain During the Great Patriotic War of 1941–1945.* 2 vols. Moscow: Foreign Languages Publishing House, 1957.

Montefiore, Simon Sebag. *Stalin: The Court of the Red Tsar.* New York: Alfred A. Knopf, 2004.

Official Kremlin International News Broadcast. "Press Conference with Veterans of the Russian Foreign Intelligence Service." Federation of American Scientists. November 18, 2003. https://fas.org/irp/world/russia/teheran43.html.

O'Sullivan, Adrian, *Espionage and Counterintelligence in Occupied Persia (Iran): The Success of the Allied Secret Services, 1941–45,* New York: Palgrave Macmillan, 2015.

———. *Nazi Secret Warfare in Occupied Persia (Iran): The Failure of the German Intelligence Services, 1939–45.* New York: Palgrave Macmillan, 2014.

Paehler, Katrin. *The Third Reich's Intelligence Services: The Career of Walter Schellenberg*. Cambridge, UK: Cambridge University Press, 2017.

Payne, Robert. *The Life and Death of Adolf Hitler*. New York: Praeger, 1973.

Plutenko, Iurii, and Gevork Vartanian, "Tegeran-43: 'My byli ne takie! . . . ,'" *Zavtra*, October 31, 2007. https://zavtra.ru/blogs/2007-10-3122.

———. "Tehran-43: Wrecking the Plan to Kill Stalin, Roosevelt and Churchill." *RIA Novosti*, October 16, 2007. https://web.archive.org/web/20120629234011/http://en.rian.ru/analysis/20071016/84122320.html.

Reilly, Michael F. *Reilly of the White House*. New York: Simon & Schuster, 1947.

Rezun, Miron. *The Soviet Union and Iran: Soviet Policy in Iran from the Beginnings of the Pahlavi Dynasty until the Soviet Invasion in 1941*. Geneva: Stijthoff & Noordhoff International Publishers, 1981.

Roll, David L. *The Hopkins Touch: Harry Hopkins and the Forging of the Alliance to Defeat Hitler*. Oxford: Oxford University Press, 2013.

Roosevelt, Franklin D. "'Day of Infamy' Speech: Joint Address to Congress Leading to a Declaration of War Against Japan." December 8, 1941. SEN 77A-H1, Records of the United States Senate, Record Group 46, National Archives. www.archives.gov/historical-docs/day-of-infamy-speech.

———. *The Public Papers and Addresses of Franklin D. Roosevelt.* Compiled by Samuel I. Rosenman. 13 vols. New York: Random House, 1938–1950.

Sainsbury, Keith. *The Turning Point: Roosevelt, Stalin, Churchill, and Chiang Kai-shek, 1943: The Moscow, Cairo, and Tehran Conferences.* New York: Oxford University Press, 1985.

Schellenberg, Walter. *Hitler's Secret Service (The Labyrinth).* Translated by Louis Hagen. New York: Harper & Row, 1971.

Scott, James M. "The Untold Story of the Vengeful Japanese Attack after the Doolittle Raid." *Smithsonian Magazine,* April 15, 2015. www.smithsonianmag.com/history/untold-story-vengeful-japanese-attack-doolittle-raid-180955001.

Sherwood, Robert E. *Roosevelt and Hopkins: An Intimate History.* New York: Harper & Brothers, 1948.

———. *The White House Papers of Harry L. Hopkins,* Vol. 2: *January 1942–July 1945,* London: Eyre & Spottiswoode, 1949.

Shoumatoff, Elizabeth. *FDR's Unfinished Portrait: A Memoir.* Pittsburgh, PA: University of Pittsburgh Press, 1990.

Skorzeny, Otto. *My Commando Operations: The Memoirs of Hitler's Most Daring Commando.* Translated by David Johnston. Atglen, PA: Schiffer Publishing, 1995.

———. "My Rescue of Mussolini, 12 September 1943." Mataxis Collection, USASOC History Office Classified Files. Fort Bragg, NC.

———. *Skorzeny's Special Missions: The Memoirs of Hitler's Most Daring Commando*. Minneapolis, MN: Zenith Press, 2011.

Smith, Jean Edward. *FDR*. New York: Random House, 2007.

Smith, Stuart. *Otto Skorzeny: The Devil's Disciple*. New York: Bloomsbury USA, 2018.

Stephan, Robert W. *Stalin's Secret War: Soviet Counterintelligence Against the Nazis, 1941–1945*. Lawrence: University Press of Kansas, 1995.

Sudoplatov, Pavel, Anatoli Sudoplatov, Jerrold L. Schecter, and Leona P. Schecter, *Special Tasks: The Memoirs of an Unwanted Witness—a Soviet Spymaster*. Boston: Little, Brown, 1994.

Thompson, Walter H. *Assignment: Churchill*. Toronto: McLeod, 1955.

———. *Beside the Bulldog: The Intimate Memoirs of Churchill's Bodyguard*. London: Apollo, 2003.

Toland, John. *The Rising Sun: The Decline and Fall of the Japanese Empire, 1936–1945*. New York: Modern Library, 2003.

Tolischus, Otto David. *Through Japanese Eyes*. New York: Reynal & Hitchcock, 1945.

Tully, Grace. *FDR: My Boss*. Chicago: People's Book Club, 1949.

West, Nigel. *Historical Dictionary of World War II Intelligence*. Lanham, MD: Scarecrow Press, 2007.

———. *Encyclopedia of Political Assassinations*. Lanham, MD: Rowman & Littlefield, 2017.

Wires, Richard. *The Cicero Spy Affair: German Access to British Secrets in World War II*. Westport, CT: Praeger, 1999.

Yenne, Bill. *Operation Long Jump: Stalin, Roosevelt, Churchill, and the Greatest Assassination Plot in History*. Washington, DC: Regnery History, 2015.

SOURCE NOTES

Prologue

Roosevelt's journey to the Soviet embassy: For the details of Roosevelt's travel from the American embassy to the Soviet embassy on this day, see Michael F. Reilly, *Reilly of the White House* (New York: Simon & Schuster, 1947), 178–79; and Gary Kern, "How 'Uncle Joe' Bugged FDR," *Studies in Intelligence* 47, no. 1 (March 2003). See also Keith Sainsbury, *The Turning Point: Roosevelt, Stalin, Churchill, and Chiang Kai-shek, 1943: The Moscow, Cairo, and Tehran Conferences* (New York: Oxford University Press, 1985), 218–19.

Shortly after the United States entered the war, the world press began to refer to Roosevelt, Churchill, and Stalin as the "Big Three."

Assassination plot: Our book will examine some debates and controversies surrounding the story of this assassination plot, including theories that the plot was exaggerated by the Soviet intelligence services. For examples of introductory sources about the story that are reliable, according to our research, see Reilly, *Reilly of the White House*, 178–88; Nikolai Dolgopolov, *Vartanian: zhizn' zamechatel'nykh liudei* (Moscow: Molodaia gvardiia, 2014), 25–73; and Iurii Kuznets, *Tehran-43* (Moscow: Eskimo, 2003), 7–10.

Fascism: Kershaw, *To Hell and Back: Europe 1914–1949* (New York: Penguin, 2015), 228–232.

Nazi persecution of the Jewish people: Kershaw, *ibid*, 356–373.

Tehran Conference: For the general significance of the 1943 Tehran Conference to World War II, see, for example, Sainsbury, *Turning Point*; and Keith Eubank, *Summit at Teheran: The Untold Story* (New York: William Morrow, 1985).

Chapter 1

"picked up a . . .": Robert E. Sherwood, *Roosevelt and Hopkins: An Intimate History* (New York: Harper & Brothers, 1948), 430–431.

"like the Japanese have . . .": Knox as quoted in Jean Edward Smith, *FDR* (New York: Random House, 2007), 536.

"one strong new idea . . .": Adolf Hitler speech of February 1940, as quoted in *St. Louis Star and Times*, February 24, 1940.

"enemy of all law . . .": Franklin D. Roosevelt, fireside chat, September 11, 1941, FDR Presidential Library and Museum, www.fdrlibrary.marist.edu/_resources/images/msf/msf01445.

"if George Washington were alive today . . .": J. Wheeler-Hill speech at Madison Square Garden in New York, February 20, 1939. Rosenfeld, Gavriel D., and Ward, Janet, Ed., *Fascism in America, Past and Present* (Cambridge: Cambridge University Press, 2023), 149.

"fight for a Gentile America . . .": Leland V. Bell, "The Failure of Nazism in America: The German American Bund, 1936–1941," *Political Science Quarterly* 85, no. 4 (December 1970): 585–599, at p. 594.

"Lending war equipment is . . .": Susan Dunn, *1940: FDR, Willkie, Lindbergh, Hitler—the Election amid the Storm* (New Haven, CT: Yale University Press, 2013), 286.

Percentage of Americans opposed to American involvement: Gallup Poll, April 28, 1941. Survey #234K, Question #8a.

Chapter 2

"It would not do this country . . .": Roosevelt to Japanese Ambassador Admiral Kichisaburo Nomura, quoted in Smith, *FDR*, 513.

"Yesterday, December 7, 1941 . . .": Franklin D. Roosevelt, "'Day of Infamy' Speech: Joint Address to Congress Leading to a Declaration of War Against Japan," December 8, 1941, SEN 77A-H1, Records of the United States Senate, Record Group 46, National Archives, https://www.archives.gov/milestone-documents/joint-address-to-congress-declaration-of-war-against-japan.

"The attack yesterday on . . .": ibid.

"I believe that I interpret . . .": ibid.

"between the United States . . .": ibid.

Chapter 3

"You ask, what is . . .": The full text of this speech is available online; see Winston Churchill, "Blood, Toil, Tears and Sweat: First Speech as Prime Minister to the House of Commons, May 13, 1940," International Churchill

Society, https://winstonchurchill.org/resources/speeches/1940-the-finest-hour/blood-toil-tears-sweat.

"I have nothing to . . .": ibid.

Other European nations, such as Ireland, Portugal, Spain, Sweden, and Switzerland, remained neutral for the duration of the war.

"Yes, the Japanese attacked . . .": David L. Roll, *The Hopkins Touch: Harry Hopkins and the Forging of the Alliance to Defeat Hitler* (Oxford: Oxford University Press, 2013), 161–62.

"the greatest joy . . .": Churchill, quoted in Smith, *FDR*, chapter 23.

Chapter 4

The full name of the USSR's army was the Workers' and Peasants' Red Army—it is better known as the Red Army.

"slapped his thighs with . . .": Nigel Hamilton, *The Mantle of Command: FDR at War, 1941–1942* (Boston: Houghton Mifflin Harcourt, 2014), 88.

"caught up in an . . .": ibid.

Ribbentrop's reaction: ibid.

Chapter 5

Iran's name: Many Europeans and Americans at the time incorrectly referred to the nation of Iran as "Persia." The preference of the Iranian government was for "Iran."

"The SD were unable to give them . . .": Security Service, KV 2/1479-1, 48.

"The situation inside the country . . .": Franz Mayr diary entry, June 28, 1942, Security Service, KV 2/1482-2, 8.

"the life of an enemy . . .": Franz Mayr diary entry, September 11, 1942, Security Service, KV 2/1482-2.

Chapter 6

"The entire area for . . .": *New York Times*, January 27, 1943.

"These conferences have discussed . . .": Roosevelt and Churchill press conference, January 24, 1943, in Casablanca, Morocco. Full transcript is from Franklin D. Roosevelt, *The Public Papers and Addresses of Franklin D. Roosevelt*, comp. Samuel I. Rosenman, vol. 12, *The Tide Turns: 1943* (New York: Harper & Brothers, 1949), 37–45.

"I think we have all had it in . . .": ibid.

"The elimination of German . . .": *ibid.*

Churchill's reaction: Recollection of John McCrea, quoted in Nigel Hamilton, *Commander in Chief: FDR's Battle with Churchill, 1943* (Boston: Houghton Mifflin Harcourt, 2016), 128–129.

"does not mean the . . .": *The Tide Turns,* 37–45.

"Well, one thing I should . . .": ibid.

"the forces ranged against us . . .": The full text of the speech is available online; see Winston Churchill, "Address to Joint Session of US Congress, 1941," America's National Churchill Museum, accessed September 10, 2021, www.nationalchurchillmuseum.org/churchill-address-to-congress.html.

"stark naked and . . .": This anecdote is widely attributed to Harry Hopkins; see, for example, Robin Renwick, *Fighting with Allies: America and Britain in Peace and War* (Hull, UK: Biteback Publishing, 2017), chapter 5.

"the Prime Minister of . . .": Renwick, *Fighting with Allies,* chapter 5.

"until we have procured the . . .": Roosevelt and Churchill press conference, January 24, 1943, in Casablanca, Morocco, 1943, *The Tide Turns,* 37–45.

"We have only to kick . . .": As quoted in Antony Beevor, *The Second World War* (New York: Little, Brown, 2012), 190.

Chapter 8

"the most unprecedented and . . .": United Press International newswire story as printed in, for example, *Richmond Times-Dispatch,* January 27, 1943. The *Times-Dispatch*'s headline was typical: "Roosevelt Flies to Africa to Talk War with Churchill: Allied Leaders Map Full 1943 Campaign to Eliminate Axis."

"No one has been a more . . .": Churchill radio broadcast on the Soviet-German war, June 22, 1941. For the complete speech, see www.jewishvirtuallibrary.org/churchill-broadcast-on-the-soviet-german-war-june-1941.

"I know you will not . . .": Roosevelt to Churchill, March 18, 1942, in Beevor, *Second World War,* 281.

Chapter 9

"I walked out of his office . . .": Walter Schellenberg, *Hitler's Secret Service,* trans. Louis Hagen (New York: Harper & Row, 1971), 29–30.

"the eternal subhumans . . .": Richard Breitman, *The Architect of Genocide: Himmler and the Final Solution* (New York: Alfred A. Knopf, 1991), 59.

"the offensive force which . . .": Leslie Alan Horvitz and Christopher Catherwood, *Encyclopedia of War Crimes and Genocide* (New York: Facts on File, 2006), 199.

"Untouched by any pangs of . . .": Schellenberg, *Hitler's Secret Service,* 30.

"total solution to the . . .": The original documents from the Wannsee Conference, including the full list of attendees, were obtained after the war by the US government, translated, and presented as evidence in the trials at Nuremberg. The paperwork, known as the "Wannsee Protocol," is archived online by the University of Pennsylvania at www.writing.upenn.edu/~afilreis/Holocaust/wansee-transcript.html.

"In the course of the final solution . . .": "Wannsee Protocol." (No page numbers are indicated in the documents as translated.)

"Since it is opportunity . . .": Adolf Hitler, as quoted in Callum MacDonald, *The Killing of Reinhard Heydrich: The SS "Butcher of Prague"* (New York: Da Capo Press, 1998), 182.

Chapter 10

"They shot any man . . .": From the diary of Father Wendelin Dunker, a Catholic missionary stationed in the region. Quoted from James M. Scott, "The Untold Story of the Vengeful Japanese Attack after the Doolittle Raid," *Smithsonian Magazine,* April 15, 2015, www.smithsonianmag.com/history/untold-story-vengeful-japanese-attack-doolittle-raid-180955001.

"These Japanese troops . . .": Gen. Chiang Kai-shek cable to Roosevelt, April 28, 1943, in Otto David Tolischus, *Through Japanese Eyes* (New York: Reynal & Hitchcock, 1945), 197.

"Get Yamamoto . . .": Craig Nelson, *Pearl Harbor: From Infamy to Greatness* (New York: Scribner & Sons, 2016), 395.

Chapter 11

Casablanca mistake: Doris Kearns Goodwin, *No Ordinary Time: Franklin and Eleanor Roosevelt: The Home Front in World War II* (New York: Simon & Schuster, 1994), 401–2. For a more detailed account of the "casa blanca" mishap and Walter Schellenberg's role in it, see Ladislas Farago, *The Game of the Foxes: The Untold Story of German Espionage in the United States and Great Britain during World War II* (New York: Bantam Books, 1973), 722–24.

Chapter 13

"an Irishman who sometimes . . .": Reilly, *Reilly of the White House,* 7.

"Traditionally American Presidents are . . .": ibid., 15.

"shivers in the . . .": ibid., 8.

"engaged in combat with . . .": "Japanese Admiral Killed in Combat," *New York Times,* May 21, 1943.

"Would you care to . . .": Presidential press conference in the Executive Office of the President, May 21, 1943, FDR Library, Marist College, www.fdrlibrary.marist.edu/_resources/images/pc/pc0149.pdf.

Chapter 14

Gevork Vartanian: For the most complete biography of Vartanian, see Dolgopolov's *Vartanian*. For short, English-language biographies of Vartanian and his activities in Tehran, see Nikolai Dolgopolov, "How 'the Lion and the Bear' Were Saved," *Russia Beyond the Headlines*, November 29, 2007, www.rbth.com/articles/2007/11/29/lion_and_bear.html; "Gevork Vartanyan," *Telegraph* (UK), January 11, 2012, www.telegraph.co.uk/news/obituaries/9008287/Gevork-Vartanyan.html; and "Russian Spy Who 'Changed the Course of History,' Goar Vartanyan, Dies Aged 93," Reuters/ABC, November 28, 2019, www.abc.net.au/news/2019-11-28/female-russian-spy-goar-vartanyan-dies-age-93/11745228.

"This name stuck . . .": Dolgopolov, *Vartanian*, 53–54.

Chapter 15

"There were times when . . .": Schellenberg, *Hitler's Secret Service*, 214–218.

Schellenberg's special precautions: ibid.

"My desk was like . . .": ibid.

"as clever or . . .": Otto Skorzeny, *My Commando Operations: The Memoirs of Hitler's Most Daring Commando*, trans. David Johnston (Atglen, PA: Schiffer Publishing, 1995), 91.

Chapter 16

Roosevelt's letter: Roosevelt to Stalin, May 5, 1943, in *Foreign Relations of the United States: Diplomatic Papers: The Conferences at Cairo and Tehran, 1943* (Washington, DC: United States Government Printing Office, 1961), 3–4.

"It is my thought . . .": ibid.

"You and I . . .": ibid.

"Therefore, I suggest . . .": ibid., 4.

"Three is a crowd . . .": Elizabeth Kimball MacLean, *Joseph E. Davies: Envoy to the Soviets* (Westport, CT: Praeger, 1992), 100.

Notes on White House meeting: Sherwood, *Roosevelt and Hopkins*, 563.

"We, both of us . . .": Churchill address to the House of Representatives, May 19, 1943, Congressional Record, vol. 89, pt. 4, 4621.

Chapter 18

"unequivocally devoted to . . .": Eubank, *Summit at Teheran*, 80–81.

Stalin's reaction: ibid.

"You are doing a . . .": Roosevelt to Stalin, May 5, 1943, in *Conferences at Cairo and Tehran*, 5.

"I think your President . . .": Eubank, *Summit at Teheran*, 82.

"seemed to be . . .": Davies to Roosevelt, May 21, 1943, in *Conferences at Cairo and Tehran*, 5.

"I agree with you . . .": Stalin to Roosevelt, May 26, 1943, in *Conferences at Cairo and Tehran*, 6–7.

"If you agree to . . .": ibid.

"As to the place . . .": ibid.

"Joe, you have . . .": Eubank, *Summit at Teheran*, 88.

"In the Mediterranean . . .": Roosevelt and Churchill to Stalin, June 2, 1943, in Susan Butler, ed., *My Dear Mr. Stalin: The Complete Correspondence of Franklin D. Roosevelt and Joseph V. Stalin* (New Haven, CT: Yale University Press, 2006), 136–38.

"the concentration of forces . . .": ibid.

"Your delay creates . . .": Stalin to Churchill and Roosevelt, June 11, 1943, in Ministry of Foreign Affairs of the USSR, *Correspondence Between the Chairman of the Council of Ministers of the USSR and the Presidents of the USA and the Prime Ministers of Great Britain During the Great Patriotic War of 1941–1945*, vol. 2 (Moscow: Foreign Languages Publishing House, 1957), 70–71.

"I quite understand your . . .": Churchill to Stalin, June 19, 1943, in Butler, *My Dear Mr. Stalin*, 141–42.

"You say that you . . .": Stalin to Churchill, June 24, 1943, in *Correspondence Between the Chairman*, vol. 2, 74–76.

"we British were left . . .": Churchill to Stalin, June 27, 1943, in *Correspondence Between the Chairman*, vol. 2, 140–41.

"I am satisfied that . . .": ibid.

"Therefore, the reproaches which . . .": ibid.

"I must emphasize . . .": W. Averell Harriman and Elie Abel, *Special Envoy to Churchill and Stalin, 1941–1946* (New York: Random House, 1975), 216–17.

"Averell told me . . .": Churchill to Roosevelt, June 25, 1943, in *Conferences at Cairo and Tehran*, 10–11.

"The whole world is . . .": ibid.

"I do not underrate . . .": ibid.

"I did not suggest . . .": Roosevelt to Churchill, June 28, 1943, in *Conferences at Cairo and Tehran*, 11.

"Of course, you and I . . .": ibid.

Chapter 19

"These meetings . . .": Schellenberg, *Hitler's Secret Service*, 354.

"We succeeded in . . .": ibid., 359.

Chapter 20

"In addition to our . . .": Roosevelt to Stalin, June 16, 1943, in Butler, *My Dear Mr. Stalin*, 141.

"Two years ago tomorrow by . . .": Roosevelt to Stalin, June 22, 1943, in Butler, *My Dear Mr. Stalin*, 144.

"It wasn't a battle . . .": Statement of Vasilii Bryukhov, Russian T-34 Commander, as quoted in Lloyd Clark, "The Largest Tank Battle in History Began 75 Years Ago Today—Here's How It Changed WWII," *Military Times*, July 5, 2018, www.militarytimes.com/veterans/military-history/2018/07/05/the-largest-tank-battle-in-history-began-75-years-ago-today-heres-how-it-changed-wwii.

Casualty numbers: These casualties include those of Operation Citadel, the Battle of Kursk, and the subsequent Soviet counterattacks. For a breakdown of these statistics, see Karl-Heinz Frieser, *Die Ostfront 1943/44: Der Krieg im Osten und an den Nebenfronten* (Munich: Deutsche Verlags-Anstalt, 2011), 153–54, 197–201; and G. F. Krivosheev, ed., *Soviet Casualties and Combat Losses in the Twentieth Century*, trans. Christine Barnard (Philadelphia: Stackpole Books, 1997), 124–32.

"Although I have . . .": Roosevelt to Stalin, July 15, 1943, in *Conferences at Cairo and Tehran*, 16.

Orel population: Figures are from Butler, *My Dear Mr. Stalin*, 149.

"Sincere congratulations to . . .": Roosevelt to Stalin, August 5, 1943, in Butler, *My Dear Mr. Stalin*, 149.

"Thank you for your . . .": Stalin to Roosevelt, August 8, 1943, in *Conferences at Cairo and Tehran*, 18.

"I have at the . . .": ibid.

"I consider that a . . .": ibid.

"I do not have . . .": ibid.

Chapter 21

"I must say . . .": Skorzeny, *My Commando Operations*, 203.

"state of wild . . .": Otto Skorzeny, *Skorzeny's Special Missions: The Memoirs of Hitler's Most Daring Commando* (Minneapolis, MN: Zenith Press, 2011), 101.

Skorzeny summons: ibid., 102.

"I . . . trembled in . . .": ibid., 109.

Chapter 22

"Now I was to . . .": ibid., 110–11.

"His word, his bearing . . .": Skorzeny, *My Commando Operations*, 230.

"The other gentlemen . . .": Skorzeny, *Skorzeny's Special Missions*, 113.

"We must find out . . .": Skorzeny, *My Commando Operations*, 229–30.

"The longer Hitler spoke . . .": Skorzeny, *Skorzeny's Special Missions*, 115.

"I have full . . .": Skorzeny, *My Commando Operations*, 230.

"I fully understand . . .": Skorzeny, *Skorzeny's Special Missions*, 115.

Chapter 23

"actively participating in German activities . . .": Security Service, KV 2/1478–4, 2.

Chapter 24

"We wish to . . .": Roosevelt and Churchill to Stalin, August 18, 1943, in *Conferences at Cairo and Tehran*, 20–21.

"I entirely share . . .": Stalin to Roosevelt and Churchill, August 24, 1943, in *Conferences at Cairo and Tehran*, 22.

"I hope you . . .": Roosevelt to Churchill, August 26, 1943, in *Conferences at Cairo and Tehran*, 23.

"A large-scale buildup . . .": Roosevelt and Churchill to Stalin, August 25, 1943, in Ministry of Foreign Affairs of the USSR, *Correspondence Between Stalin, Roosevelt, Truman, Churchill and Attlee during World War II* (Honolulu, HI: University Press of the Pacific, 2001), 150–51.

"Nothing is nearer . . .": This speech is reprinted at length in the Australian newspaper *The Morning Bulletin*. Please see "Broadcast by Churchill from Quebec: 'Drive On Until We Have Finished the Job,'" *Morning Bulletin*, September 2, 1943, 1, 4, https://trove.nla.gov.au/newspaper/article/56288916/5448880. The speech can also be listened to at the International Churchill Society website, https://winstonchurchill.org/resources/speeches/1941-1945-war-leader/broadcast-from-quebec.

"I still hope . . .": Roosevelt to Stalin, September 4, 1943, in *Conferences at Cairo and Tehran*, 23.

"As to our . . .": Stalin to Roosevelt, September 8, 1943, in *Conferences at Cairo and Tehran*, 24.

"Legation" refers to a diplomatic office of lower rank than an embassy, headed by a minister rather than an ambassador. The distinction between the two ceased to be used after World War II.

Chapter 25

"Pick fifty men . . .": Skorzeny, *Skorzeny's Special Missions*, 120.

"It was certain . . .": Otto Skorzeny, "My Rescue of Mussolini, 12 September 1943," Mataxis Collection, USASOC History Office Classified Files, Fort Bragg, NC.

Operation Eiche preparations: "Operation Eiche: The Rescue of Benito Mussolini," *Veritas* 11, no. 1 (2015): 37.

"Helmets on!": Skorzeny, *Skorzeny's Special Missions*, 189.

"The pilot turned . . .": ibid.

"Crash landing . . .": ibid., 191.

Chapter 26

"I am delighted . . .": Roosevelt to Stalin, September 11, 1943, in *Stalin's Correspondence*, 92–93.

"I am pleased . . .": Churchill to Stalin, September 10, 1943, in *Stalin's Correspondence*, 161.

"I am therefore . . .": ibid.

"As regards the meeting . . .": Stalin to Roosevelt and Churchill, September 12, 1943, in *Stalin's Correspondence*, 94.

"Then perhaps only . . .": Churchill to Stalin, October 1, 1943, in *Stalin's Correspondence*, 165–66.

"The code name for . . .": ibid.

"I do not think . . .": Stalin to Churchill, October 3, 1943, in *Stalin's Correspondence*, 170–71.

Chapter 27

"I closed my eyes . . .": Skorzeny, *Skorzeny's Special Missions*, 190.

Plane crash: ibid.

"stick to him . . .": ibid., 191.

"A hasty kick . . .": ibid., 191–95.

"My eyes swept the . . .": ibid.

"Duce, the Führer . . .": ibid.

Takeoff details: Skorzeny, *Skorzeny's Special Missions*, 202–3.

"You have performed . . .": Hitler's words to Skorzeny, as quoted in Skorzeny, *Skorzeny's Special Missions*, 202–3.

Chapter 29

Arrest of Franz Mayr: "Narrative of the Arrest of Franz Mayr," Security Service, KV 2/1478.

Chapter 30

"Unfortunately, not one of . . .": Stalin to Roosevelt, October 19, 1943, in Butler, *My Dear Mr. Stalin*, 174.

"I would have to travel . . .": Roosevelt to Stalin, October 21, 1943, ibid., 178.

Chapter 31

"Cordell Hull is in . . .": Reilly, *Reilly of the White House*, 160–63.

"Whatever he has . . .": ibid.

"Because the Boss . . .": ibid.

"Good luck, Mike . . .": ibid.

Chapter 32

For figures and information on *Erntefest* or Operation Harvest Festival, see Yitzhak Arad, *The Operation Reinhard Death Camps: Belzec, Sobibor, Treblinka: Revised and Expanded Edition* (Bloomington: Indiana University Press, 2018), chapter 46; and Stefan Klemp, *"Aktion Erntefest": Mit Musik in den Tod: Rekonstruction eines Massenmords* (Münster: Geschichtsort Villa ten Hompel, 2013).

"I did not regard . . .": Heinrich Himmler quoted in Ian Kershaw, *Hitler, 1936–1945: Nemesis* (London: W. W. Norton, 2000), 876–77.

"The United Kingdom . . .": "Joint Four-Nation Declaration," October 1943, at Yale Law School's The Avalon Project: Documents in Law, History and Diplomacy, https://avalon.law.yale.edu/wwii/moscow.asp.

Chapter 33

"The whole world . . .": Roosevelt to Stalin, November 8, 1943, in *Conferences at Cairo and Tehran*, 72.

"I thank you for . . .": Stalin to Roosevelt, November 10, 1943, in *Conferences at Cairo and Tehran*, 78.

"I now feel that . . .": Churchill to Roosevelt, October 27, 1943, in *Conferences at Cairo and Tehran*, 48.

"We have had . . .": Churchill to Roosevelt, October 20, 1943, in *Conferences at Cairo and Tehran*, 34.

"This is not . . .": Eubank, *Summit at Teheran*, 139.

"must have been . . .": ibid., 141.

Chapter 34

"I could see that . . .": Schellenberg, *Hitler's Secret Service*, 333–34.

Cicero's photographs: Elyesa Bazna, aka "Cicero," later wrote a memoir detailing his exploits; see Elyesa Bazna, *I Was Cicero*, trans. Eric Mosbacher (New York: Harper & Row, 1962).

"his documents speak . . .": Schellenberg, *Hitler's Secret Service*, 333–34.

"I'll repay you . . .": Slava Katamidze, *Loyal Comrades, Ruthless Killers: The Secret Services of the USSR, 1920's to the Present* (New York: Lewis International, 2003), 105.

Chapter 35

"seething with unrest . . .": Reilly, *Reilly of the White House*, 164.

"filled with Axis . . .": ibid.

"The air raid defense . . .": ibid.

"before and during the . . .": ibid.

Reilly's inspection: Reilly, *Reilly of the White House*, 172. Reilly refers to the NKVD chief he meets as "General Artikov," but independent scholar Gary Kern suggests it was more likely General Dmitri Arkadiev, who headed the NKVD's department of transportation and was apparently present at the conference. See Kern, "How 'Uncle Joe' Bugged FDR."

American legation location: In his memoir, Reilly incorrectly cites the distance as four miles. Reilly, *Reilly of the White House*, 174.

"the Germans have . . .": Reilly, *Reilly of the White House*, 175.

Germans in the mountains: ibid.

"The German parachutists could . . .": ibid.

"We extended the protected . . .": ibid.

"Russian, British and American . . .": ibid.

Chapter 36

Underground water tunnels: See Iurii Plutenko and Gevork Vartanian, "Tegeran-43: 'My byli ne takie! . . . ,'" *Zavtra* (October 31, 2007), https://zavtra.ru/blogs/2007-10-3122.

Chapter 37

"As we approached the . . .": Churchill, *The Second World War*, vol. 5, *Closing the Ring* (London: Cassell, 1952), 302.

"four or five . . .": Churchill, *Closing the Ring*, 302.

"There was no kind . . .": ibid.

"I grinned at the . . .": ibid.

Chapter 38

"captured some of . . .": Reilly, *Reilly of the White House*, 177.

"thirty-eight Nazis had . . .": ibid.

"The way he said . . .": ibid.

"disclosed that there were . . .": ibid.

"for the President to . . .": ibid.

Chapter 39

"received bad news . . .": Harriman and Abel, *Special Envoy*, 263.

"There might be an . . .": ibid.

"Even if it . . .": ibid.

"a most unfortunate . . .": ibid.

"I pressed him within . . .": ibid.

"Although the furnishings were . . .": ibid.

Chapter 40

Stalin and Molotov's message: Harriman to Roosevelt, as recorded in "The President's Log at Tehran," in *Conferences at Cairo and Tehran*, 463.

"The risk of assassination . . .": ibid.

"bring the three heads . . .": ibid.

"we would be responsible . . .": ibid.

"it was Stalin who . . .": Harriman and Abel, *Special Envoy*, 264.

"Stalin and Churchill would . . .": Reilly, *Reilly of the White House*, 177–78.

"If anything happens . . .": ibid.

"Do you care which . . .": ibid.

Chapter 41

"I had no stomach . . .": ibid., 178.

"We lined the entire . . .": ibid.

"As soon as the . . .": ibid.

"tearing through the . . .": ibid.

"The Boss . . . was vastly amused . . .": ibid., 179.

Chapter 42

"I'll talk to him . . .": ibid.

"Stall him a . . .": ibid.

"Seeing him for the . . .": ibid.

"His hair was . . .": John L. Bates, "The 'Eureka' Conference: A Busy Time in Teheran," *Military Review*, 66, no. 10 (October 1986): 78.

"He was a small . . .": Reilly, *Reilly of the White House*, 179.

"sort of amble[s] across . . .": ibid., 179–80.

"At last!": Charles E. Bohlen, *Witness to History, 1929–1969* (New York: W. W. Norton, 1973), 139.

Roosevelt's photograph suggestion: Bates, "'Eureka' Conference," 78–80.

"I take pleasure in welcoming those present . . .": "Proceedings of the Conference, Sunday, November 28, First Plenary Meeting (Combined Chiefs of Staff minutes)," in Conferences at Cairo and Tehran, 497.

Chapter 43

"an immense expedition . . .": "Proceedings of the Conference, Sunday, November 28, First Plenary Meeting (Bohlen minutes)," in *Conferences at Cairo and Tehran*, 489.

"We cannot do . . .": "Proceedings of the Conference, Sunday, November 28, First Plenary Meeting (Combined Chiefs of Staff minutes)," in *Conferences at Cairo and Tehran*, 499.

"he and the . . .": "Proceedings of the Conference, Sunday, November 28, First Plenary Meeting (Bohlen minutes)," in *Conferences at Cairo and Tehran*, 489.

"The best method in . . .": ibid., 490.

"of great importance in . . .": "Proceedings of the Conference, Sunday, November 28, First Plenary Meeting (Combined Chiefs of Staff minutes)," in *Conferences at Cairo and Tehran*, 501.

"long agreed with the . . .": ibid.

"some of the . . .": "Proceedings of the Conference, Sunday, November 28, First Plenary Meeting (Bohlen minutes)," in *Conferences at Cairo and Tehran*, 492.

"Overlord be accepted as . . .": "Proceedings of the Conference, Sunday, November 28, First Plenary Meeting (Combined Chiefs of Staff minutes)," in *Conferences at Cairo and Tehran*, 505.

Chapter 44

"fourteen or sixteen . . .": Plutenko and Vartanian, "Tegeran-43."

"We wanted to . . .": ibid.

"loaded with weapons.": Dolgopolov, *Vartanian*, 36.

"had readied a villa . . .": Plutenko and Vartanian, "Tegeran-43."

"we recorded their . . .": Iurii Plutenko and Gevork Vartanian, "Tehran-43: Wrecking the Plan to Kill Stalin, Roosevelt and Churchill," *RIA Novosti*, October 16, 2007, https://web.archive.org/web/20120629234011/http://en.rian.ru/analysis/20071016/84122320.html.

"preparing to land a . . .": ibid.

"the assassination or . . .": ibid.

"The second group . . .": ibid.

Chapter 45

"I shall insist on . . .": Averell Harriman's recollection of Churchill's words, as quoted in Robert E. Sherwood, *The White House Papers of Harry L. Hopkins* (London: Eyre & Spottiswoode, 1949), vol. 2, 779.

"the most important and . . .": "Proceedings of the Conference, Sunday, November 28, First Plenary Meeting (Bohlen minutes)," in *Conferences at Cairo and Tehran*, 537.

"Stalin kept needling . . .": Harriman and Abel, *Special Envoy*, 273.

"Several times through the . . .": ibid.

"would rise again within . . .": "Proceedings of the Conference, Monday, November 29, Tripartite Dinner Meeting (Bohlen minutes)," in *Conferences at Cairo and Tehran*, 553.

"that some 50,000 . . .": Bohlen, *Witness to History*, 147.

"The British Parliament and . . .": Harriman and Abel, *Special Envoy*, 274.

"Fifty thousand must . . .": Churchill, *Closing the Ring*, 330.

"I would rather be . . .": ibid.

"I'd like to go . . .": Churchill quoted in Eubank, *Summit at Teheran*, 316.

Chapter 46

"assassination or abduction of . . .": Plutenko and Vartanian, "Tehran-43."

"It was tempting to . . .": ibid.

Chapter 47

"fighting a losing battle . . .": Bohlen, *Witness to History*, 148.

"We will launch Overlord . . .": Foreign Relations of the United States: Diplomatic Papers, The Conferences at Cairo and Tehran, 1943, J. C. S. Files *Combined Chiefs of Staff Minutes*, November 30, 1943, 9:30 a.m., Department of State, Office of the Historian. https://history.state.gov/historicaldocuments/frus1943CairoTehran/d369.

"Stalin, who had waited . . .": Harriman and Abel, *Special Envoy*, 274.

"Now that the decision . . .": "Third Plenary Meeting, November 30, 1943 (Bohlen minutes)," in *Conferences at Cairo and Tehran*, 577.

"transfer troops from the . . .": ibid.

"cover plan . . . to confuse . . .": ibid., 578.

"truth deserves a . . .": ibid.

Chapter 48

Stalin's entrance: Eubank, *Summit at Teheran*, 343.

"a man who has devoted . . .": "Tripartite Dinner Meeting, November 30, 1943 (Boettiger minutes)," in *Conferences at Cairo and Tehran*, 583.

"Stalin the Great . . .": Harriman and Abel, *Special Envoy*, 276.

"the honors which . . .": "Tripartite Dinner Meeting, November 30, 1943 (Boettiger minutes)," in *Conferences at Cairo and Tehran*, 583.

"his joy in the . . .": ibid.

"We have differing customs . . .": Bohlen, *Witness to History*, 150.

Chapter 51

"the repository and . . .": Churchill, *Second World War*, vol. 1: *The Gathering Storm* (Boston: Houghton Mifflin, 1948), 10.

"a dozen submachine-guns . . .": Stuart Smith, *Otto Skorzeny: The Devil's Disciple* (New York: Bloomsbury USA, 2018), 231–32.

Chapter 52

"He said they had . . .": Averell Harriman, quoted in Adrian O'Sullivan, *Espionage and Counterintelligence in Occupied Persia (Iran): The Success of the Allied Secret Services, 1941–45* (New York: Palgrave Macmillan, 2015), 182. See also Harriman and Abel, *Special Envoy*, 264–65.

Walter Thompson: See Walter Thompson's memoirs, Walter H. Thompson, *Assignment: Churchill* (Toronto: McLeod, 1955), esp. p. 283, and *Beside the Bulldog: The Intimate Memoirs of Churchill's Bodyguard* (London: Apollo, 2003).

Beria's account: For the full Beria account of Tehran, see Beria, *Beria, My Father: Inside Stalin's Kremlin*, ed. Françoise Thom, trans. Brian Pearce (London: Duckworth, 2001), 92–5. Beria further claims Stalin required him to do the same for the Yalta conference; see Beria, *Beria, My Father*, 103–6. Another Soviet agent, Zoya Zarubina, also claims she was assigned to gather information on Roosevelt and his entourage at Tehran and Yalta, playing the role of a hostess and furnishing Roosevelt's Tehran villa; see Inez Cope Jeffery, *Inside Russia: The Life and Times of Zoya Zarubina: Former Soviet Intelligence Officer and Interpreter During the Stalin Years* (Austin, TX: Eakin Press, 1999), 1–25.

"I believe that . . .": Skorzeny, *My Commando Operations*, 204.

"the plan was simply . . .": ibid.

"resisted interrogation with . . .": Adrian O'Sullivan, *Nazi Secret Warfare in Occupied Persia (Iran): The Failure of the German Intelligence Services, 1939–45* (New York: Palgrave Macmillan, 2014), 124.

Chapter 53

"We have learned that . . .": "Fourth Inaugural Address of Franklin D. Roosevelt," Saturday, January 20, 1945, at Yale Law School's The Avalon Project: Documents in Law, History and Diplomacy, https://avalon.law.yale.edu/20th_century/froos4.asp.

"I have a terrific . . .": Elizabeth Shoumatoff, *FDR's Unfinished Portrait: A Memoir* (Pittsburgh, PA: University of Pittsburgh Press, 1990), 174–75.

"I felt as if I . . .": Churchill, *Second World War*, vol. 6: *Triumph and Tragedy* (Boston: Houghton Mifflin, 1953), 471.

"overwhelmed by a sense . . .": ibid.

"The child patients . . .": Grace Tully, *FDR: My Boss* (Chicago: People's Book Club, 1949), 369.

INDEX

20 Pages TK

ACKNOWLEDGMENTS

FROM BRAD

This book became far more personal than we expected. So let me start by thanking the one person whose point of view so deeply matches my own, Josh Mensch. When it comes to writing a book together, it helps to share ideas—but it's far more helpful when you also share a similar worldview and values. Josh and I have been working together for nearly a decade now, which means that my original impression was absolutely correct: He is one of the kindest, most thoughtful people I've ever encountered—and one of the most thorough researchers and writers, committed to sourcing every bit of history that's packed into these pages. Yet, as with each book we do together, something new emerges, and here, it was his dedication to making sure that the victims of this war—from the Jews in the Holocaust to the civilians who were starved and plowed over—were never excluded from the story. As a Jewish writer myself, I'd grown up learning about the Holocaust, but as the research took us deeper, we were both still humbled to see this new view of the decimation, including the utterly bureaucratic process that empowered and enabled the Nazi horrors. *How did this happen?* we still ask today. Sadly, the answer is: *Quite easily.* So, Josh, thank you for always seeing what's vital—both today and yesterday. I'm honored to call you and Mary my friends. This book would never exist without you.

I also owe massive thanks to the following: My first lady, Cori, who has helped me find, redefine, and build my own history. Jonas, Lila, and Theo are my own Big Three, the reason for it all. They are a united front against their parents, and I hope it'll always be that way. I'm writing these acknowledgments after the passing of my friend and agent, Jill Kneerim, the single most important person in my professional life. No words are enough. I love and miss you dearly. Friend and agent Jennifer Rudolph Walsh built this nonfiction universe—and Jay Mandel at WME has run so beautifully with it. Special thanks to Hope Denekamp, Lucy Cleland, and all our friends at the Kneerim & Williams agency.

I want to also thank my sister, Bari, who knows my history like no one else. Also to Bobby, Ami, Adam, Gilda, and Will, for always looking out for us.

My Secret Service holds my life in their hands: Noah Kuttler, Ethan Kline, Dale Flam, Matt Kuttler, Chris Weiss, and Judd Winick are always there to keep me honest—and every page is improved by it. Additional thanks go to Chris Eliopoulos, Katy Greene, Marie Grunbeck, Nick Marell, Staci Schecter, Liz Sobel, Caryn Stumpfl, Pansy and Rob Price, Jason Sherry, Jim Day, Denise Jaeger, Katriela Knight, and Maria Venusio.

For research and historical support, we are so grateful to have Jeff Alexander on our Allied front. His insights and expertise are interwoven throughout these pages. Thank you, Jeff, for guiding us along the way. Special thanks to our incredible researchers, Benjamin Diehl and Garret McDonald, who are our true secret weapons.

Massive love to our family at *Lost History*, and at

HISTORY and Left/Right, for bringing Josh and me together all those years ago: Nancy Dubuc, Paul Cabana, Mike Stiller, Ken Druckerman, Mike Mezaros, Mary Robertson (who is also family!), and Lee White; and to Rob Weisbach, for being the first to say yes.

I also want to thank everyone at Scholastic: Lisa Sandell, Elizabeth Parisi, Cianna Sanford, and the entire team. And everyone at Flatiron and Macmillan: our leader and friend Don Weisberg, Jon Yaged, Kristen Bonanno, Marlena Bittner, Aileen Boyle, Nancy Trypuc, Vincent Stanley, Emily Walters, Donna Noetzel, Jeremy Pink, and Keith Hayes, as well as Astra Berzinskas, Malati Chavali, Leigh George, Jenn Gonzalez, Jonathan Hollingsworth, Laura Pennock, Brad Wood, Jeanette Zwart, plus Jasmine Faustino, Lauren Bittrich, and the entire sales force. I'll never say it enough: They're the real reason this book is in your hands.

I need to add a special thank-you to the unstoppable Louis Grilli, who kept the trains running, then put the trains on his back and carried us into the final station, saving us on a nearly daily basis. Especially toward the end. Thank you, Louis! Finally, I want to thank our true Commander in Chief, Bob Miller. As we've said in other books, leadership isn't about being in charge—it's about taking care of those in your charge. Bob, you constantly take care of us. Your friendship and passion brought this series to fruition. I owe you forever for this chapter of my life. Thank you, Bob, for your faith.

FROM JOSH

First, I want to thank Brad Meltzer. Brad and I have worked together for a decade now, and the stories we've told have spanned centuries. Brad, it's been a remarkable journey writing with you, and your emphasis on kindness and generosity in work and life remains an inspiration. Thank you, truly, for being a great collaborator and friend. As always, Mary and I send our love to you and Cori and your wonderful family.

Brad and I owe an enormous debt of gratitude to Bob Miller at Flatiron Books. From the beginning, Bob's support, encouragement, and commitment have been the engine that drives us. We also owe thanks to many other great people at Flatiron who make our work possible. At the top of this list is Louis Grilli, who contributed so much to this book from start to finish. Louis, we couldn't have done this without you! Thanks also to Nancy Trypuc, Marlena Bittner, Katherine Turro, and the many great folks on the sales team, the marketing team, the audiobook team, and so many others. Shout out also to Jasmine Faustino and Lauren Bittrich, whose work was so important to our earlier books.

I want to give a very special thank-you to my agent, Lisa Grubka, at Fletcher & Company. During a difficult and stressful time, Lisa provided much-needed guidance and wisdom. Lisa, thank you for your patience and encouragement every step of the way.

When it came to helping unravel the strands of this enormously complicated story, two people were essential: researchers Benjamin Diehl and Garret MacDonald. Ben, thank you for helping me navigate the dense maze of conflicting sources in the early stages of the process; and Garret, thank you for your outstanding input, organization, and guidance in the final stretch. This story is ours together. I also must thank our wonderful editor, Jeff Alexander, whose sure-handed input made this book so much better. Thanks also to my brother, James Freeman, for providing some excellent translations from Russian to English. Working together with such smart and dedicated people was one of the absolute highlights of this project.

As authors of nonfiction history, we rely completely on the organizations that preserve and document historical materials for public and scholarly use. For this project I want to thank, among many other institutions, the Franklin D. Roosevelt Presidential Library at Marist College, the United States Holocaust Memorial Museum, the National World War II Museum, and the New York Public Library.

I also want to thank my extended family. The writing of this book coincided with a painful time for us, and I'll forever associate the work with this difficult period. Despite the loss, we found together a camaraderie and generosity with one another that I'll never forget. In that spirit I want to thank Greg Patnaude, Pamela Mensch, Elizabeth Mensch, Jonathan Mensch, Jacob Mensch, Joseph Mensch, James Freeman, Jeremy Freeman, Libby Mensch, and Claire Mensch. I also want to thank Anna Acunto, John Acunto, London Acunto, Mila Acunto, and August Acunto, Lynn James, Daeon James, and Denae James.

My deepest gratitude of all is for my two children,

Malcolm and Maxine, who bring new laughter and joy every single day. You make me the proudest father in the world. Finally, throughout every trial and every triumph, one person has remained my foundation: my wife, Mary Robertson. Thank you for being my best friend and soul mate. I love you forever.

ABOUT THE AUTHORS

Brad Meltzer is the Emmy-nominated, #1 *New York Times* bestselling author of *The Lightning Rod, The Escape Artist, The Lincoln Conspiracy, The JFK Conspiracy, The First Conspiracy, Heroes for My Daughter, Heroes for My Son,* and many other bestselling thrillers, as well as the Ordinary People Change the World series. He is also the host of the History Channel TV shows *Brad Meltzer's Decoded* and *Brad Meltzer's Lost History,* which he used to help find the missing 9/11 flag that the firefighters raised at Ground Zero. A graduate of the University of Michigan and Columbia Law School, Brad lives with his family in Florida. Visit Brad Meltzer online at bradmeltzer.com.

Josh Mensch is a *New York Times* bestselling author and documentary television producer with a focus on American history. He is coauthor with Brad Meltzer of *The First Conspiracy*, *The JFK Conspiracy*, *The Nazi Conspiracy,* and *The Lincoln Conspiracy.* For television he has written, directed, and produced nonfiction series for PBS, the History Channel, and other networks. He lives in Brooklyn, New York, with his family.